"Our world is a mixed bag when it comes to encouragement. Often, words meant to inspire overwhelm us with burdensome demands: *be better, work harder, do more*. We need a better encouragement. Thankfully, Lindsey Carlson's book offers the remedy we need by speaking life-giving truths from God's word to God's people."

**Melissa B. Kruger,** Director of Women's Content, The Gospel Coalition; author, *Growing Together*

"We live in a paradoxical time: it seems women are more discouraged than ever, but at the same time, peppy self-help talk abounds, printed on every throw pillow and journal cover in the home decor section. Our steady diet of 'you've got this' does not actually fill us up. In *A Better Encouragement*, Lindsey Carlson shows us how we were made to find hope, comfort, and strength in the much deeper and richer promises of God. This book offers a timeless truth especially poignant for this cultural moment: the deepest need of discouraged women is not self-confidence but the confident assurance of our identity in Christ. I commend this book to any weary woman and all her friends."

**Jen Oshman,** author, *Enough about Me* and *Cultural Counterfeits*

"'I'm so discouraged' is a sentence that comes out of my mouth more often than I would like. And, as a pastor's wife, it's one I also hear frequently—Christian women everywhere, weighed down by the trials of life, are struggling to take heart. Thankfully, in this book, Lindsey Carlson establishes weak hearts by pointing us to the source of true courage: God himself. With clarity, biblical depth, and a refreshing sprinkle of wry humor, *A Better Encouragement* reveals our God to be the hope, comfort, and strength we desperately need. Whether you are enduring a day or a decade of faint-hearted weariness, I'd encourage you to find help in these pages."

**Megan Hill,** author, *Praying Together* and *A Place to Belong*; Managing Editor, The Gospel Coalition

"Lindsey Carlson gives us a compelling biblical vision for the encouragement we long for and offer to others. Ultimately the courage, confidence, and hope that we all desperately need won't be found in the self-help aisle but in God himself. *A Better Encouragement* rebooted a passion in me to be a better encourager."

**Kathy Litton,** Director of Planter Spouse Development, North American Mission Board

*A Better Encouragement*

# A Better Encouragement

*Trading Self-Help for True Hope*

Lindsey Carlson

WHEATON, ILLINOIS

*A Better Encouragement: Trading Self-Help for True Hope*

Copyright © 2022 by Lindsey Carlson

Published by Crossway
      1300 Crescent Street
      Wheaton, Illinois 60187

Cover design: Crystal Courtney

First printing 2022

Printed in the United States of America

All Scripture quotations are from the ESV® Bible (The Holy Bible, English Standard Version®), copyright © 2001 by Crossway, a publishing ministry of Good News Publishers. Used by permission. All rights reserved.

All emphases in Scripture quotations have been added by the author.

Paperback ISBN: 978-1-4335-7771-0
ePub ISBN: 978-1-4335-7774-1
PDF ISBN: 978-1-4335-7772-7
Mobipocket ISBN: 978-1-4335-7773-4

---

**Library of Congress Cataloging-in-Publication Data**

Names: Carlson, Lindsey, 1982- author.
Title: A better encouragement : trading self-help for true hope / Lindsey Carlson.
Description: Wheaton, Illinois : Crossway, 2022. | Includes bibliographical references and index.
Identifiers: LCCN 2021049792 (print) | LCCN 2021049793 (ebook) | ISBN 9781433578038 (paperback) | ISBN 9781433578045 (pdf) | ISBN 9781433578052 (mobipocket) | ISBN 9781433578069 (epub)
Subjects: LCSH: Christian women–Religious life. | Encouragement–Religious aspects–Christianity.
Classification: LCC BV4527 .C275 2022 (print) | LCC BV4527 (ebook) | DDC 248.8/43–dc23/eng/20211118
LC record available at https://lccn.loc.gov/2021049792
LC ebook record available at https://lccn.loc.gov/2021049793

---

Crossway is a publishing ministry of Good News Publishers.

| BP | | | | | | | | | | | |
|----|----|----|----|----|----|----|----|----|----|----|----|
| BP | | 30 | 29 | 28 | 27 | 26 | 25 | 24 | 23 | 22 | |
| 14 | 13 | 12 | 11 | 10 | 9 | 8 | 7 | 6 | 5 | 4 | 3 | 2 | 1 |

*To the women of*
*Imprint Community Church*

*I praise God for your friendship and encouragement.*
*Thank you for walking beside me as I've learned to love and*
*value biblical encouragement within the local church.*
*May grace and peace be multiplied to you.*

# Contents

# Introduction

DO YOU APPRECIATE ENCOURAGEMENT? I do. In fact, I could always use a little more. I love opening my mailbox to find an encouraging note inside. I enjoy a nod of affirmation when I've worked hard on a project or my prayers or counsel help someone. And when trials come and life isn't easy, it's nice when a thoughtful friend stops by with flowers. I've always appreciated receiving encouragement.

But encouragement is utilized and enjoyed by people everywhere, not just inside the church and not only by those who follow Jesus. Culturally, we're all taught very early in life to expect positive affirmation and use reward-based motivation. We all like it and we all use it.

We learn the powerful sway of encouragement from our very first days on earth. Parents clap when their baby takes her first steps or says his first words. Teachers punctuate their students' schoolwork with stickers and gold stars in order to affirm a job well done or praise extra effort. Encouragement strengthens children for growth and maturity. At every age and stage, we've learned to appreciate encouragement because of its ability to advance us forward in everything from being on time, to eating healthy, to getting a good night's sleep, and onto the tougher, more difficult challenges.

Encouragement has the potential to deliver an enormous measure of love and support when we are struggling. We appreciate the assurance that someone notices our difficulty or our success and cares enough to say something. Encouragement reminds us that we are seen, known, and loved. When we're down, encouragement feels like good medicine. It affirms our gifts and abilities and keeps us focused and committed to our daily work. And when our work is finished, who doesn't appreciate a final pat on the back?

With how much we all tend to like and appreciate encouragement, you'd think that we would all have naturally become expert encouragers who freely provide encouragement to others. We certainly have plenty of opportunities each day to see people, just like us, who want encouragement like us, and to do unto others as we'd have them do unto us. So why don't we speak up? Why aren't we all walking, talking, ever-flowing fountains of encouragement? When we see the kindness of the grocery store clerk or the patience of the teenager's AP calculus teacher or the generosity of a friend who took the time to listen, why don't we say something encouraging?

In twenty years of women's ministry, not one woman has ever confessed to me that she simply had too much encouragement in her life. Quite the opposite is true. I frequently hear Christian women lamenting a lack of encouragement. Yet, encouragement is a tool often utilized by God throughout the Old and New Testaments to strengthen and exhort his people for the difficult road ahead. When we look today at the scores of underencouraged women in our churches, we must consider whether or not we are personally prepared to encourage one another (1 Thess. 4:18) as members within the larger body of Christ.

If we desire more encouragement—or better encouragement—we should assume others probably do too. But when we aren't accustomed to regularly feeling encouraged or trusting that encouragement is readily available when we need it, we get tired of waiting and give up on looking for it. The more desirous we become as we wait for a kind word or a hint of support, the more we worry that no one wants to help. Like David in Psalm 142:4, we may look around and think: "There is none who takes notice of me; no encouragement remains for me! No one cares for my soul." But for Christians, this simply isn't true; those who fear the Lord have no lack (Ps. 34:9).

I began studying the subject of encouragement in Scripture because I recognized what appeared to be an existing need within the church. Everywhere I went, in big churches and small ones, women craved encouragement. And yet, even among Christians I spoke to, there seemed to be a gap between the personal desire for better encouragement and the practical know how. Many of us aren't sure how to effectively encourage one another, partly because we can't define it. If we can't define encouragement, we can't adequately provide it. And when we are not skilled encouragers, we will unintentionally withhold the good gift of encouragement from others within our local church. But when Christians learn to generously provide encouragement that honors Christ, God strengthens his people and his church simultaneously.

Better encouragement exists. This book aims to help you find it by providing scriptures, cultural observations, and diagnostic questions to assist you as you seek to grow in wisdom and discernment. *A Better Encouragement: Trading Self-Help for True Hope* is organized into nine chapters. In each chapter, we will examine the desires and longings that are intended to drive Christians to God's encouragement and how the self-help industry has filled our hearts and minds with lesser substitutes. Then, we will look at how God hears the cries of his people, provides better promises, and meets real needs with his encouragement.

In chapter 1, we'll further examine the need for encouragement and establish a working definition of "better encouragement." In chapters 2 through 4 we will observe how an overemphasis on self-esteem, self-sufficiency, and self-empowerment have prevented us from relying on the God of encouragement (chapter 2) to provide the substance of encouragement (chapter 3) in order that we might depend on the power of encouragement (chapter 4). In chapters 5 through 7 we will see how the encouragement of strength (chapter 5), encouragement of comfort (chapter 6), and encouragement of hope (chapter 7) offer a better message than that preached by the self-help industry. Finally, in chapter 8 we will observe how God simultaneously encourages his people and builds his church through the unity of encouragement.

Sister, I commend you to the merciful riches of Christ, who has secured a better encouragement for you than anything this world has to offer.

# 1

# The Reason for Encouragement

"DO YOU FEEL ENCOURAGED?"

My friend's cheerful question hung unanswered in the air over our empty latte mugs. I grasped aimlessly for a socially appropriate answer to avoid the truth. "Encouraged?" I repeated the word in the form of a question. Had I heard her correctly? I tried not to appear caught off guard by her inquiry, but I wondered if she'd even been listening over the past hour as I'd recounted the highlights of my tumultuous year.

I thought about how much my life had been turned upside down since we'd last seen one another. Our family had moved across the country from Texas to Maryland in order to plant a church in a state where we knew almost no one. Leaving the only state I'd ever lived in and living far away from grandparents, aunts, uncles, cousins, and friends felt painful and lonely. A month after our move, God surprised us with the news of baby number five. In a season where I already felt exiled, rootless, foreign, and alone, I'd also faced another difficult pregnancy, a stint of bed rest, and then another round of postpartum depression. To say I was encouraged was a stretch.

Of course, that morning in the coffee shop, I conveyed only the high points and the signs of God's blessing. I wanted my heart to be content and rejoice in all things, so I worked to maintain that image in our conversation. When my life didn't fit the glowing narrative of exemplary faith, I simply skipped over reporting the signs of trouble or my existing fears as though they didn't exist. But as I edited integral portions of the story, I painted an overly rosy picture of our reality. I smoothed out the rough edges of a year where I'd felt smothered by the weight of discouragement. My hope hadn't just been deferred, it had dried up. The cares of my heart were many.

Puritan pastor and author Richard Sibbes explains, "the sighs of a bruised heart carry in them a report, both of our affection to Christ, and of his care for us."[1] I wasn't eager to hit publish on such a grim report but I also didn't know how to positively spin the news of my spiritual discouragement. My friend repeated her question: "Do you feel encouraged?"

If I was being honest I would have said, "No, not really. I'm actually pretty discouraged. Here's how you can pray for me." But I didn't. Instead, I simply nodded and smiled, even though I was discouraged and my heart was filled with lament. If I had provided my friend with a more honest report, it would have sounded like the weary confession of Jeremiah in Lamentations 3:17–18: "My soul is bereft of peace; I have forgotten what happiness is; so I say, 'My endurance has perished; so has my hope from the Lord.'"

---

1   Richard Sibbes, *The Bruised Reed* (Edinburgh: Banner of Truth Trust, 2018), 66.

## Defining Discouragement

You may be wondering why I would begin a book on encouragement with a chapter on discouragement. I admit, it's kind of a Debbie Downer move. But don't worry, this is a book about encouragement. Yet, before we are able to discuss encouragement, we must be prepared to recognize the precipitating need that exists inside each and every one of us and leads us all to desire encouragement: *discouragement.* We are a people who grow weary and are easily discouraged by trials and difficulty.

In Deuteronomy 1:21, the Lord instructs Moses to command his people to go in and establish the land that he has given them, saying, "Go up, take possession, as the LORD, the God of your fathers, has told you. Do not fear or be dismayed." We are familiar with fear, but what about dismay? The original Hebrew word is *hatat,* which means to be prostrated, broken down, or discouraged. Whether literally broken down by violence or figuratively by confusion and fear,[2] to be *hatat* is to be deprived of courage or confidence, hindered by disfavor, or dissuaded from doing something.[3] When we are discouraged, our spirit is broken down.

In the Old Testament, the Israelite people provide a vivid picture of aimless, wandering discouragement. Even after God delivered his people from Egypt, provided food and water in the desert, and made promises assuring Israel of their certain victory over the land and their enemies, Israel still managed to struggle with dismay. They were too easily discouraged and doubtful of God's promises and goodness. All the wandering and heat had

---

2 *Blue Letter Bible,* "חָתַת," accessed September 4, 2021, https://www.blueletterbible.org/.

3 *Merriam-Webster,* s.v. "discourage (*v.*)," accessed September 4, 2021, https://www.merriam-webster.com/.

beaten them down, hindered them with the fear of God's disfavor, and robbed them of courage to continue on. But although we tend to interpret their discouragement as glaring faithlessness, God didn't write them off. He implored them not to fear or be discouraged. He provided good words of counsel to his people because he saw their weariness and anticipated the costliness of discouragement.

You may have picked up this book because you are currently in a season of discouragement. Or, maybe you're not. Whether today, tomorrow, or next year, you will face discouragement at some point. It might be minor or major; it may begin in your home, your job, your relationships, or your church community. Wherever you are, no matter your age, stage, or spiritual maturity, opportunities for discouragement abound over the course of life. Here's why: (1) you are a weak and broken sinner, (2) you are pursued by an enemy, and (3) you live in a broken world filled with sin and suffering. Discouragement is a reality for us all because we are not the Lord, who "does not faint or grow weary" (Isa. 40:28). But God, the Creator of the ends of the earth, is prepared for your weariness.

Encouragement isn't just a likable concept; it's a resource and a learnable skill that, for Christians, is worthy of pursuit. When your heart has been prostrated and broken down, you need solutions and strategies that will help you in the moment and heal and strengthen you for the days ahead. When you don't hold editorial privilege over every aspect of your life and story, God encourages you to look for his unfolding grace. He masterfully authors every detail of your life for your good. He kindly reveals himself in the midst of human weakness in order to strengthen and encourage those who love him. God promises and provides the good encouragement his people need to endure.

Discouragement tempts us to abandon the good work set before us or give up too soon when life gets hard or when hope seems dim. As a child, Thomas Edison's teacher believed that the man who we now know as America's greatest inventor was too stupid to learn anything. One of Walt Disney's editors reportedly said that Disney "lacked imagination and had no good ideas."[4] Think of how these discouraging sentiments could have significantly stifled the brilliance and creativity of two vital contributors to our society. Instead, they endured scrutiny and negative feedback, and the light of truth and beauty prevailed. Edison and Disney didn't believe their bad press; they continued to think, create, and labor, and eventually the work of their hands spoke for itself. God created each of his children to labor faithfully and fruitfully in his kingdom. He has given you gifts and strengths that he intends to use within the story he's written; your life is filled with worth and value that displays the goodness of God in unique ways. You can't give up every time you grow weary of doing good. You are called to faithfully endure seasons of discouragement, trusting that God is at work in you as you labor joyfully within his kingdom.

Imagine how different the church would be today if Noah, Moses, Joshua, John the Baptist, or any of the disciples or early church members had surrendered to their discouragement and given up on serving and obeying God or carrying forth the gospel message. Because God encouraged them along the way, his church

4   Alana Horowitz, "15 People Who Were Fired Before They Became Filthy Rich," *Business Insider*, April 25, 2011, https://www.businessinsider.com/.

has been sustained throughout the years. God encourages and sustains his people too.

## Why Do Believers Need a Book on Better Encouragement?

Early on in the process of writing this book, an older believer asked me if Christians really needed to be taught and exhorted on the subject of biblical encouragement. She was unconvinced. Did Christian women doubt their need for help? Did they struggle to find encouragement from God or from one another? Did they actually misunderstand biblical encouragement?

In my experience, yes, yes, and yes. I've spent almost twenty years as a pastor's wife, loving and serving discouraged Christian women inside various local churches, and yes—many Christian women are unaware of their own discouragement. Yes, many Christian women struggle to find the encouragement they long for. And yes, many discouraged Christian women are unsure of how and where to begin their search for encouragement. I have also been one of these discouraged and fruitlessly searching women.

Many of the discouraged women who I've been privileged to know and encourage both love and follow Jesus. And yet, even though they are born-again believers, they struggle to apply the hope of the cross to the weariness of their soul. When they face discouragement, they are often too worried that their trial will be scrutinized, their theology corrected, or their weakness exploited to come and admit their need for encouragement. This needs to change.

Sisters, before we can find better encouragement or become better encouragers, we must understand our basic need of encouragement. We need encouragement because we are easily discouraged. Each one of us. We are tempted to grow weary of doing good and to give up too soon. When we are bruised and broken, we must often be convinced to get up one more time and to strengthen our weak muscles and make straight paths for our feet. I pray this book convinces you to get up and keep going by helping you to find better encouragement.

When you face new or ongoing discouragement, still marked and scarred by old wounds, you may be tempted to take your unmet needs away from God, the church, and other Christians. You may have been hurt or disappointed by discouragement in your past and falsely blamed God or his people for not hearing or answering your cries in the ways that you'd hoped. But stepping away from the Lord's provision, the fellowship of your local church, or the presence of spiritually mature believers who love you will surely end in greater heartache and trouble. In making the choice to step away from God, his word, his people, the weekly worship gathering, or the divine sacraments Christ provided as a means of common grace, you choose to depart from the path God designed to lead you to encouragement.

Today it seems as though we need permission to feel discouraged and to trust God to provide exactly what we need. Consider the condition of Elijah in 1 Kings 19:4–8 when he fled to the wilderness to preserve his life, took shelter under the broom tree, and begged in his discouragement for God to take his life because his suffering was too much. While the Lord didn't take Elijah's suggested course of action, he did refresh Elijah's weariness of soul. When Elijah felt unable to press on, God provided a physical place for him to rest and sleep. He sent an angel to counsel him. He gave him a cake to eat and a jar of water for him to drink. Only then did God instruct Elijah to arise and go in strength.

Christians need a book on better encouragement because we are weary and tired of hanging on to hope. We need to be refreshed by being reminded of how to meet our basic needs for encouragement. We need discipleship and accountability and a chance to practice better encouragement inside our relationships and our local church. But before we can begin, we must start with the work required within our own heart. So before we go any further, let me ask you the question my friend asked me: Are you encouraged?

## Why Are You Downcast?

Where are the signs of discouragement in your own life? Where has life left you prostrated or broken down? How are you tempted to give up too quickly? We are often uncomfortable with considering or questioning the longings of our soul when we need not be. The psalmist specifically inquires of his own heart, "Why are you cast down, O my soul, and why are you in turmoil within me?" (Ps. 43:5).

When you are frustrated, disappointed, or discouraged, do you allow yourself the freedom and the space to consider the state of your spirit and confess any areas of festering discouragement to God? Or do you regard discouragement as something to be ashamed of or that needs to be kept hidden? Take note of how you tend to approach your own discouragement. Some of us overlook it. Some hide it. Some notice but attempt to ignore it. And some of us become overly concerned with its presence and try to manage or fix it on our own. None of these approaches are the healthiest way of addressing existing needs—because they all seek a remedy apart from God.

In Psalm 142, when David is frustrated, overwhelmed, and discouraged after fleeing from King Saul, he laments that his good friend has now become his vindictive enemy. And he does so by turning to God in the midst of his desperation. He cries, "In the path where I walk they have hidden a trap for me. Look to the right and see: there is none who takes notice of me; no refuge remains to me; no one cares for my soul" (Ps. 142:3–4). David feels afraid, alone, and utterly hopeless in his discouragement. When we are discouraged, are we willing to confess every part of the story to God, even if it's uncomfortable or embarrassing?

We can't expect that identifying or confessing discouragement will immediately rectify the pain. Our desire to escape heartache and discomfort is understandable. But it is stubborn and idealistic for Christians to cling to the belief that they can work around or escape suffering. This is a troubling trend that concerns Christian author Joni Eareckson Tada. She explains, "It's a different era now. Many young people I know . . . [believe suffering] should be mitigated at all costs. And if it cannot be avoided, it must be drugged, divorced, escaped from, or prayed away."[5]

Eareckson Tada was permanently paralyzed in a diving accident at the age of seventeen and has spent her life confined to a wheelchair. By God's strength, she has taught his word, spoken at conferences across the world, written books (she's published over forty-eight!), and carried the good news of the gospel to the

5   Joni Eareckson Tada, foreword to *Becoming Elisabeth Elliot*, by Ellen Vaughn (Nashville: B&H Publishing, 2020), xiv.

disabled community for over forty years.[6] Instead of succumbing to a life of passivity, watching Netflix on the couch, Joni fixed her eyes on Jesus. When she couldn't walk away from suffering, she found herself being carried by Christ. Her endurance, kingdom-minded labor, and joy are all spiritual fruit. When we don't have the choice to sidestep pain, suffering, or discouragement, we can always trust that God is in the process of writing a beautiful story of redemption.

On the fiftieth anniversary of her accident and paralysis, Eareckson Tada reflected on the Lord's mercy:

> Decades of study, paralysis, pain, and cancer have taught me to say, "It was good for me to be afflicted so that I might learn your decrees" (Ps. 119:71). I won't rehearse all of suffering's benefits here. . . . The process is difficult, but affliction isn't a killjoy; I don't think you could find a happier follower of Jesus than me. . . . God shares his joy on his terms only, and those terms call for us to suffer, in some measure, like his Son. I'll gladly take it.[7]

As God allowed Joni Eareckson Tada periods of discouragement— crushing and pressing her in painful, extraordinary trials—he refined and purified her, filled her life with good fruit, and made her heart overflow with true and lasting joy in Christ.

### Read the Good Report

In Numbers 13, the weary Israelites are wandering in the wilderness, grumbling and complaining to Moses who is probably

---

6   Joni and Friends, https://www.joniandfriends.org.
7   Joni Eareckson Tada, "Reflections on the 50th Anniversary of My Diving Accident," *The Gospel Coalition*, July 17, 2019, https://www.thegospelcoalition.org/.

getting discouraged from listening to them, when God seeks to provide everyone with a bit of encouragement. He calls Moses to commission the twelve heads of the tribes of Israel to go into the land as reconnaissance spies and gather intelligence. The twelve spies are tasked with taking note of what they find and then bringing back a report.

Scripture notes that the men go out during the "season of the first ripe grapes," the beginning of the fruit-bearing season (Num. 13:20). If the men gathered any fruit on this expedition, they could expect an even bigger harvest months later once they moved in and all the trees were in full production. As Moses sends the men off, he exhorts them to "be of good courage and bring some of the fruit of the land" (Num. 13:20) because he knows that presence of fruit should be a morale booster for everyone.

The spies find good fruit, cut down a branch with a single cluster of grapes, and bring pomegranates and figs from the Valley of Eshcol. But they don't seem too excited about their spoils. For some reason, the evidence of fruit in the land is not enough to adequately convince them to trust that God has indeed gone before them, prepared a good land for their inheritance, and filled it with fruit-bearing trees for them to eat from. Rather than returning with a glowing report that boasts in God's faithfulness, the men return with doubts and hesitations and end up providing the people with a bad report even though they're holding the tangible fruit that God intends for their encouragement right in their hot little hands. What an oversight!

God could have used the men's testimony of his faithfulness to encourage and stir up all twelve tribes and to joyfully lead them forward in victory as they laid hold of the land he had promised.

But instead, the men overlook the fruit in the land (Num. 13:23), get hung up on the details, and are sidetracked by their own fears. Like any skilled worrier might do, they made a pros and cons list citing all their concerns:

| Pros | Cons |
| --- | --- |
| milk, honey, limited selection of fruit | strong current residents, fortified cities, Anak's scary relatives are there |

As they faced the facts, they deemed the threat too great even though God had already promised to go before them and to give their enemies into their hand. When Israel's leaders were asked to walk by faith in the promises of God, they ignored the good report God had given them and constructed a fictional one to worry about instead. Classic.

## The Dangers of Discouragement

Fruit is a sign of God's faithfulness to his people. Each grape of the vine could have provided strength. If only the twelve spies had filled their report with all the existing good news, this good word would have made them glad (Prov. 12:25). A good report of the land could have strengthened God's people to rejoice in his provision and encouraged them to move faithfully forward. But the twelve men's doubts effectively neutralized the entire nation of Israel from obediently moving forward in the confidence of God's promise and power.

Isn't this usually the result of discouragement? When we are discouraged, we are filled with doubt, sorrow, and hopelessness and are effectively neutralized so that we will no longer be a powerful instrument of hope within the kingdom of light. The enemy who comes to steal, kill, and destroy aims to take us down and keep us out of commission and hopeless.

Discouragement threatens more than our feelings. It takes aim at our beliefs and then it attacks our actions too. When we feel discouraged, we aren't motivated to hold on to the truth of God and we give up too easily. Surrendering to our perception of discouragement may prevent us from noticing God's provision and taking comfort in him. In discouragement, we believe a bad report and fail to trust God's promises or to move forward with his help and strength. Christians need encouragement to walk by faith, pursue holiness, trust the process of sanctification when it appears too slow, and obey God when he asks them to die to self. When we are tempted to compile our own bad report and fear the coming defeat, we need God's encouragement to prevent us from giving up on the fight.

In the Christian life, we have a responsibility to be strong and courageous (Josh. 1:6) and to work out our salvation with fear and trembling for God's good pleasure (Phil. 2:12). We can't give up; we must fight the good fight (1 Tim. 6:12) and endure till the end (Heb. 12:7), enjoying the process (James 1:2) and bringing glory to God (1 Cor. 10:31). As followers of Jesus, we are called to walk faithfully before the Lord, loving him with our whole heart, mind, and strength and doing what he commands; and we trust that the God who loves us works all things together and provides good blessings and grace in our weakness. But discouragement convinces us to doubt that God's promises are true, to abandon the pursuit of his peace, and to give up on upholding his law any time it's too hard.

Discouragement also tempts us to fall into ambivalence and to disconnect from God, his word, and his people. We become tempted to isolate ourselves from our church body and withdraw from those who might see our discouragement. We may fear being seen, known, and loved by people who genuinely desire to come alongside us in discouragement and support us, holding our arms up like Aaron and Moses. Instead of trusting God to encourage us through his people, discouragement tempts us to fear that God will humiliate us, so we hide our need for help from the church in order to avoid the potential of exposure or further humiliation. When we are discouraged, we are often too afraid to afford other Christians the opportunity to know or speak into our pain.

## Lift Up Your Heart

When we are discouraged, we need the Lord to free us from the trap of our own unfruitful thinking and from the lies of the enemy because we are more easily fooled into believing that God is withholding his blessing when we are weary. But God is not waiting to relinquish his blessings based on our performance. While the enemy's desire in discouragement is to convince us that we do not have what we need and we never will, God provides encouragement that proves otherwise. In Christ we are not unseen, unheard, unloved, or alone.

Discouragement tempts us to believe that it is foolish to desire a better, easier, happier, more enjoyable, trouble-free, and pain-free existence and that to search and eagerly long for one is sinful or shameful. God's good report—in his word, people, and church—aims to set the record straight. Together, they tell the world what is indeed good and true. The Christian's desire to live in a world without suffering—where happiness and joy are our regular reality and where we are never tempted to grow weary—is a good desire. It's just not our reality yet.

When we think of heroes in the hall of faith of Hebrews 11, do we consider that each of the names in the list experienced significant trials, oppression, and discouragement? We do not conclusively label their lives as failures or their stories as ones of overarching discouragement. No, instead we see the product of their encouragement—their strong faith. When we place their discouragement in the context of the greater redemptive narrative, it gives us perspective on our own lives and helps us see that discouragement is only a piece of our story.

The stories of Moses's discouragement, Joshua's fears, and all of the disciples' affliction and persecution in the New Testament beckon us to believe the good report of God's faithfulness and to avoid the panic of our present discouragement. We can trust there's more good fruit here and in the land to come. Discouragement need not weaken our resolve when God intends to use it for the strengthening of our faith. How might God be inviting you to come to him as your Father and confess your discouragement? In his helpful book *The Bruised Reed*, pastor Richard Sibbes writes:

> It is dangerous to look for that from ourselves which we must have from Christ. . . . We are as reeds shaken with every wind. We shake at the very noise and thought of poverty, disgrace, or losses. We give in immediately. . . . We have no power over our eyes, tongues, thoughts, or affections, but let sin pass in and out. How soon we are overcome by evil, whereas we should

overcome evil with good. How many good purposes stick in the birth, and have no strength to come forth—all which shows that we are nothing without the Spirit of Christ. We see how weak the apostles themselves were, till they endured with strength from above . . . after the Spirit of Christ fell upon them, the more they suffered, the more they were encouraged to suffer. Their comforts grew with their troubles. Therefore in all, especially difficult encounters, let us lift up our hearts to Christ, who has Spirit enough for us all, in all our exigencies, and say with good Jehoshaphat, "We have no might . . . neither know we what to do: *but our eyes are upon thee.*"[8]

God loves broken, bruised, discouraged sinners. He isn't annoyed or disappointed by weakness. He's already provided encouragement for you. Behold, Christ invites you to come to him while you are still weak. Come to Jesus, who Isaiah 42:4 says "will not grow faint or be discouraged till he has established justice in the earth." He will lift every burden and carry your heart to the Father for encouragement: "There is never a holy sigh, never a tear we shed, which is lost . . . take heed of a spirit of discouragement . . . since we have so gracious a Saviour."[9]

---

8  Sibbes, *Bruised Reed*, 114–15; italics added.
9  Sibbes, *Bruised Reed*, 51.

# 2

# The God of Encouragement

ATHLETE GABRIELA ANDERSEN-SCHIESS was thirty-nine years old when she represented Switzerland at the 1984 Summer Olympics in Los Angeles as a competitor in the very first women's Olympic marathon. As she crossed the finish line, reporters snapped photographs of her glorious triumph and a stadium of supporters cheered her on to victory—even though she did not win.

The first 20 miles of the 26.2-mile course went as expected. Her difficulty began in the final 6.2 miles as the Los Angeles sun beat down, temperatures soared, and humidity hovered around 95 percent. Her body began to overheat. Her muscles cramped. As Andersen-Schiess entered the stadium, staggering and clearly in physical distress, she attempted to tackle the final 400 meters where each competitor was intended to complete the race and cross the finish line before a crowd of eager spectators. As the crowd began to notice Andersen-Schiess, many gasped and rose to their feet in concern, fixing their eyes on her wilted form.

Weaving in and out of the track's lanes, the runner's body continued to crumple: she bent forward at the waist, her head hung down, her left arm dangled limply beside her as she robotically lunged forward on locked leg muscles. Every step seemed painfully calculated. Years later she explained that though she wanted "to keep running and going straight," her "legs cramped up from lack of water" and she lost control over them.[1] She recalled, "In my spirit and my head, I knew . . . I had to go around the track and I knew where the finish line was . . . if you go to the Olympics, your goal is to finish what you came for."[2]

As she limped along, she was visibly surrounded by support. A team of doctors traveled beside her, observing her for signs of danger. If they offered her help and she accepted, she would be disqualified, so she waved them away. But the runner's active sweat and mental clarity meant she could safely continue forward. For an excruciating five minutes and forty-four seconds, thousands of standing fans clapped as their crescendoing cheers urged the runner on to victory.

When she crossed the finish line the crowd roared in a loud, unified cry of celebratory excitement and then Andersen-Schiess collapsed into the arms of waiting medics who lifted her up and carried her off the track. Though she'd placed thirty-seventh out of forty-four and hadn't won a medal, her story is remembered because of how she endured difficulty and ran faithfully all the way to the end.

---

1    "In Their Own Words: Marathon Immortality For Gutsy Andersen-Schiess," International Olympic Committee, video, March 28, 2017, 1:35, 1:44, accessed November 18, 2021, https://olympics.com/.

2    "In Their Own Words," 1:48–2:07.

## Defining How We Think about Encouragement

Hebrews 12:1 refers to Christians as spiritual runners called to "run with endurance the race that is set before us." All runners are prone to weariness. We all need support on the path of faith when our hearts are heavy and our muscles feel weak. In order to make it all the way to the finish line without succumbing to the crippling effects of spiritual dehydration, we need encouragement, not just a stadium filled with cheerleaders.

Many of us have been conditioned by our culture to desire encouragement that more closely resembles a pep squad. We want lives filled with abundant support, but we assume that to feel encouraged, we need a wealth of close personal friends who are always standing by to provide compliments and approval or who will cheer us on to strength and victory when we're not sure we are able to keep going. We want our friends and family members to be skilled encouragers and to know exactly how to cheer us on. When we don't have a loud or adoring cheer section, we worry we have no available encouragement.

But what if we had access to better encouragement all along and we just didn't recognize it? What if we'd been looking for claps and cheers from adoring fans when we should have been looking for help and courage? We often assume that we are in the position of deciding or dictating the kind of personal encouragement that we need, and then that is what we tend to seek for ourselves and provide to others.

If I asked you to encourage another Christian by texting her, what message would you send? What would you attempt to communicate? Would you compliment her on how cute her outfit looked on Sunday morning? Would you affirm her parenting by applauding her well-behaved kids? Maybe you would inspire a weary woman with words like, "You are such a rockstar. You own this day!" Perhaps you would motivate her to take more "me time" this weekend. These are all common ways I've heard women attempt to encourage each other. But is this the encouragement that Christians need the most?

When we define encouragement differently, we struggle to actually encourage or be encouraged. Encouragement feels harder than it should because we can't effectively serve one another. For Christians, encouragement doesn't need to be so difficult; we have a clearer word of instruction. When we read the same instructions and define encouragement in the same way, the entire body of Christ will be strengthened and unified and Christians will be better encouraged. God's people must all share in the same better encouragement.

How would you define encouragement? Merriam-Webster's dictionary explains that to encourage is to

- inspire with courage, spirit, or hope: HEARTEN
- attempt to persuade: URGE
- spur on: STIMULATE
- give help: FOSTER[3]

We do not typically expect enough of our encouragement. We pick one of these descriptors and call it good. We assume that as long as the words feel like a verbal gold star, the encouragement is worthy of sticking to our heart and making us feel acceptable and confident. We assume that the goal of encouragement is to feel appreciated and

3 *Merriam-Webster*, s.v. "encourage, (*v.*)," accessed September 4, 2021, https://www.merriam-webster.com/.

approved of and perhaps have our good noticed by others. With this understanding, we look for words of encouragement that

**Compliment:** by offering "a polite expression of praise or admiration"[4]

**Affirm:** by saying "something [we desire to be] true in a confident way"[5]

**Inspire:** by filling us with "the urge or ability to do or feel something"[6]

**Motivate:** by providing us with a motive or "reason to act"[7]

These are tools of the trade that we've gathered from a self-help culture that in 2019 was worth 11.6 billion dollars.[8] Christians, we haven't slipped by unscathed. We frequently tend to believe that to be complimented, affirmed, inspired, or motivated is the same as being encouraged, and that's all there is to it.

## Helping Ourselves to Encouragement

The self-help industry continues to grow every year. Some have projected that by the year 2025 it will be worth fourteen billion

4  *Merriam-Webster*, s.v. "compliment, (*v.*)," accessed September 4, 2021, https://www.merriam-webster.com/.

5  *Merriam-Webster*, s.v. "affirm, (*v.*)," accessed September 4, 2021, https://www.merriam-webster.com/.

6  *Merriam-Webster*, s.v. "inspire, (*v.*)," accessed September 4, 2021, https://www.merriam-webster.com/.

7  *Merriam-Webster*, s.v. "motive, (*v.*)," accessed September 4, 2021, https://www.merriam-webster.com/.

8  John LaRosa, "$10.4 Billion Self-Improvement Market Pivots to Virtual Delivery During the Pandemic," *Market Research* (blog), August 2, 2021, https://blog.marketresearch.com/.

dollars.[9] *Forbes* reports that millennials are shelling out nearly three hundred dollars a month on self-help products, services, and strategies that "range from new workout regimes and diet plans to life coaching, therapy and apps designed to improve wellbeing."[10] Why? Based on the women I know, it's often because we are discouraged and want to do what we can to help ourselves to happiness. The self-help industry is happy to help us invest our time, our money, and our trust.

An article in fashion magazine *Elle* promises that "whether you want to feel more courageous, implement new habits for your daily routine, stop worrying or become more productive, self-help books have the ability to help you unlock your potential, and have you feeling happier and healthier."[11] Could all of life's greatest discouragements really get better by clicking the curated affiliate links? They think so; and they provide a list of the year's best *forty-six* self-help books. Among the list of bestsellers are several book titles that rely on the use of expletives in order to offer a brand of no-nonsense encouragement that will help discouraged women supposedly get their lives together, freak-out less, and be winners who are able to accomplish more and succeed in life.

This kind of solution-based, self-help encouragement is not a phenomenon that Christian women have managed to escape. One secular news outlet noticed that when Christian author Rachel Hollis's first two books were printed by a popular Christian

9   LaRosa, "$10.4 Billion Self-Improvement Market."
10  Caroline Beaton, "Never Good Enough: Why Millennials Are Obsessed with Self-Improvement," *Forbes*, March 29, 2016, https://www.forbes.com/.
11  Katie O'Malley, "46 of the Most Inspiring Self-Help Books to Refresh the Way You Think in 2021," *Elle*, August 18, 2021, https://www.elle.com/.

publisher they "were gobbled up as gospel by a fanbase of mostly white, Christian women."[12] Both titles hit the top of the *New York Times* bestseller list; one remained there for eighty-five weeks and sold over three million copies.[13] Another secular newspaper reported that Hollis referred to her motivational encouragement as "preaching" and summarized how she'd quickly garnered her "own kind of evangelical following," which the journalist credited to Hollis's "rah-rah affirmations, confessional girl talk and folksy exclamations."[14] But when Hollis's marriage ended and her preachy positivity continued, readers became less tolerant and began to fall away.

Christian women must avoid the temptation to follow their discouragement down the cultural causeway that leads to self-help strategies. We should already know that we cannot help ourselves. In a stand-up routine, comedian George Carlin asked: "If you're looking for self-help, why would you read a book written by somebody else? . . . That's not self-help, that's help. There's no such thing as self-help. If you did it yourself, you didn't need help."[15] When a Christian lacks the courage, spirit, or hope to walk by faith, to follow God's commands, or to love God and others, she needs the help of God's encouragement—not the world's—in order to discern all that is true, good, and beautiful.

Listen to the urgency in Paul's warning to Timothy in his second letter as he pleads with him to avoid those who have the

12  Stephanie McNeal, "Rachel Hollis Is Out of Touch With the Times," *BuzzFeed News*, June 29, 2021, https://www.buzzfeednews.com/.

13  McNeal, "Rachel Hollis."

14  Allie Jones, "The No-Nonsense Gospel of Rachel Hollis," *New York Times*, March 12, 2019, https://www.nytimes.com/.

15  George Carlin, *Complaints & Grievances*, November 17, 2001, New York, NY, Atlantic.

appearance of godliness but deny its power: "For among them are those who creep into households and capture weak women, burdened with sins and led astray by various passions, always learning and never able to arrive at a knowledge of the truth" (2 Tim. 3:6–7). When we are weak, we are more easily fooled and led astray. False encouragement won't help or satisfy our hearts. The self-help movement calls women to find refreshment at an oasis that is nothing more than a mirage. Self-help isn't encouragement—it's sand.

Christian, you need not fear that when you draw near to God, his encouragement or merciful hand will disappear just like the world's offers of encouragement. Augustine wrote: "God is not a deceiver that he should offer to support us, and then, when we lean upon him, should slip away from us."[16] God is here, ready and willing to encourage you. Christian, you need encouragement that serves a better purpose than providing shallow compliments, affirming your preferences, inspiring personal bests, or motivating more lucrative sales. God's people need encouragement that lasts longer than the next thirty-day Instagram challenge and is sustained by more than the power of positive thinking.

## The Christian's Better Message: Freed from Self-Sufficiency

Encouragement based on self-confidence has produced a world of underencouraged Christians. Our confidence is too often in our own desires and feelings, both of which are subject to change. When our confidence is shaken, our heart grows quickly discouraged and we are far less likely to endure the trials set before us.

16 Francis W. Johnston, *The Voice of the Saints: Counsels from the Saints to Bring Comfort and Guidance in Daily Living* (London: TAN Books, 2003), chap. 16.

We lose the ability to stand firm, fight the good fight, and run the race set before us. But in order for encouragement to hearten, urge, stimulate, and foster courage in the heart of the Christian, the message must be applicable for us personally and reliable when our feelings aren't.

Only God is able to completely satisfy our desire for encouragement because only he is capable of fully understanding every desire of our heart and knowing how to lovingly provide exactly what we need. Think about how difficult it is to encourage others when we aren't always sure how or when we fear we might hurt instead of help. None of us can fully understand the desires of our own hearts or the hearts of others. To make matters even more complicated, our desires are a moving target.

We must be encouraged by words that do not change or fail; we require the encouragement of God's word that "proves true" and "is a shield for all those who take refuge in him" (Ps. 18:30). As worldly philosophies in our culture attempt to convince us we are good enough on our own and that happiness and joy are our own responsibility, we need God's truth to free us from the weight of this oppressive cultural lie. Christian, there is freedom in recognizing you are a limited creature who relies first and foremost on the care of your limitless Creator.

This is the good news that Jesus came to preach to weary hearts: "If you abide in my word, you are truly my disciples, and you will know the truth, and the truth will set you free" (John 8:31–32). Christ's disciples are not meant to self-produce their own courage, freedom, or good news. We must be reminded of the good news we've already been promised: Christ's "divine power has granted to us all things that pertain to life and godliness, through the knowledge of him who called us to his own glory and excellence, by which he has granted to us his precious and very great promises" (2 Pet. 1:3–4).

As Christians, when we encounter various messages meant for our encouragement, we should be able to clearly discern two distinguishing characteristics. The Christian's encouragement must be:

1. Filled with God's promises.
2. Given for the encouragement of God's people by grace through Christ.

God's encouragement frees us from the burdensome weight of our own feelings in times of discouragement and when we lack confidence. We need encouragement that points us to the unchanging truth of God. Encouragement from the triune God heartens and urges us toward his complete sufficiency and goodness, and the Spirit stimulates and fosters courage and comfort in the hearts of those who have been adopted through Christ. As God's people, we need encouragement meant specifically for the family of God. Followers of Christ are meant to be persuaded by the power of God's encouragement and his ability to provide his people with the clarity of biblically informed thinking.

## Noticed and Encouraged by God

Encouragement was God's idea first; he created it for your good before you even learned to like it. God has faithfully encouraged his people from the beginning of history. In Genesis 21:11 when Abraham's jealous wife Sarah vindictively cast Hagar and her infant son

Ishmael out into the wilderness, Abraham was "very displease[ed]." But the Hebrew word in verse 11 means more than slightly annoyed. Abraham was broken to pieces, made good for nothing, afflicted, and hurt;[17] he was too discouraged to believe God would ever fulfill his promise to make him the father of many nations.

But in Genesis 21:12–13, God bends low to encourage, saying to Abraham, "Be not displeased because of the boy and because of your slave woman. Whatever Sarah says to you, do as she tells you, for through Isaac shall your offspring be named. And I will make a nation of [Ishmael] because he is your offspring." God's words of encouragement lifted Abraham to his feet and moved his spirit forward into obedience; he "rose early in the morning and took bread and a skin of water and gave it to Hagar" and then sent her away (Gen. 21:14). Abraham was encouraged to trust and abide in God's ability to uphold his word and to rest in the assurance that he would sustain and care for Hagar and Ishmael.

Then, when Hagar's water runs out in the wilderness, it's her turn for overwhelming discouragement. She places Ishmael under the bushes, fully expecting him to die there, and sitting down, "she lifted up her voice and wept. And God heard the voice of the boy" (Gen. 21:16–17) and provided an angel that called to Hagar from heaven:

> "What troubles you, Hagar? Fear not, for God has heard the
> voice of the boy where he is. Up! Lift up the boy, and hold him
> fast with your hand, for I will make him into a great nation."
> Then God opened her eyes, and she saw a well of water. And

17 *Blue Letter Bible*, "רָעַע," accessed September 5, 2021, https://www.blueletterbible.org/.

she went and filled the skin of water and gave the boy a drink. And God was with the boy, and he grew up. (Gen. 21:17–20)

God encouraged Hagar to persevere when she'd been abandoned in the desert with an infant and lacked the water required to stay alive. He could have quietly showed her a stream or simply renewed her wilted spirit. But instead, he instructed Hagar to get up, pick up her baby, and "hold him fast." The Hebrew word for "hold" is *hazaq*, which means to cleave, take heart, be strengthened, or cling to confidence.[18] Hagar needed more than a hug or the positive thoughts of her friends from home; she needed God to stir her heart with the courage required to rise out of her despair and continue to cleave to his promises in a moment of barren wilderness. And when Hagar listened and obeyed, God opened her eyes and helped her find the water she needed for survival.

God encourages his people by pointing clearly to himself as their source of confidence. In the Old Testament the Lord moved Israel forward by the word of his promise, equipping them to walk in obedience, providing them with signs of promise, and speaking to them through the prophets. God's people had every reason to believe that he was with them and to trust that he would continue to meet their needs. One of the most frequent ways that God meets the needs of his people is by enabling their hands, feet, and voices to serve one another.

The first time that God instructs one of his people to provide encouragement to another is in Deuteronomy 1:38 when he

---

18 *Blue Letter Bible*, "חָזַק," accessed September 5, 2021, https://www.blueletterbible.org/.

told Moses to "encourage" Joshua so that Joshua would hold fast to God and courageously lead Israel into the land of their inheritance.

Moses encourages Joshua without a word of compliment and nary a positive-thinking pep talk. He doesn't inspire Joshua with his own war stories or affirmations about Joshua's natural leadership abilities. Moses obeys God's instruction to encourage Joshua by addressing him in the sight of all Israel with the words of God's promise. In Deuteronomy 31:7–8 Moses tells Joshua to "be strong and courageous" because God would "go with this people into the land that the LORD [had] sworn to their fathers to give them," and God would enable Joshua to "put them in possession of it." God's promise encouraged Joshua, not complimented or flattered him.

In Deuteronomy 1:38, when God instructs Moses to "encourage" Joshua, we find the same Hebrew word, *hazaq*. To *hazaq* Joshua meant to "causatively strengthen, to fortify, and to make strong"[19] so that, just like Hagar, Joshua could hold fast to God's promises and find the strength he needed to obediently move forward. God's promises encouraged Joshua's heart to stand firm in the face of a terrifyingly monumental task that Joshua probably knew he couldn't complete on his own. Israel's long-standing doubts, their hesitancy to move, and their downright rebellion would have likely seemed insurmountable to any levelheaded leader. Discouragement could have prostrated Joshua in the same faithless surrender. But instead, God's encouragement fortified Joshua with specific, tangible promises of help that Joshua could cleave to for support.

---

19  *Blue Letter Bible*, "חָזַק," accessed September 5, 2021, https://www.blueletterbible.org/.

Moses's words of encouragement exhorted Joshua to trust the reliable character of God who pledged his companionship to his people: "It is the Lord who goes before you. He will be with you; he will not leave you or forsake you. Do not fear or be dismayed" (Deut. 31:8). Joshua's strength wasn't intended to come from his own wisdom or might. Thus the Father's words served as a shield when Joshua turned to them for refuge. There is freedom in the simplicity of this encouragement. Moses didn't need to be positively convinced of Joshua's excellent leadership skills, talents, or ability to endure—he could encourage him by God's word of promise. And Joshua could listen and receive the encouragement of God's promise without dissecting what Moses meant or questioning Moses's fitness to encourage him. Encouragement based on God's promises removes the middleman.

When Joshua was assured of God's presence and protection by the encouragement of God's promise, he was persuaded and spurred on to obedience and action. God would go before him. God would be with him. God would not forsake him. The battle was the Lord's. When spiritual runners who are prostrated and broken down then stand, go, pick up the pace, and continue running toward victory, the audience is sure to cheer and celebrate the runner's endurance. When God is proclaimed as the source of our encouragement, strength, and hope, God receives all glory, laud, and honor after spiritual runners cross the finish line.

Discouragement is often a sign that Christians have become "dull of hearing" (Heb. 5:11); weariness has broken us down, we are not strengthened, not comforted, not cheered by the promises of God, and we need his help to stand up and start running again. In these moments and seasons, God recognizes that we often "need someone to teach [us] again the basic principles of the oracles of God" (Heb. 5:12), not in a condescending way that questioningly chides, "Why have you forgotten this?" but in a gentle way that asks like God's angel asked Hagar, "What troubles you?" In discouragement, God is always at work, listening for our cries, lifting up our hearts to his promises of relief, and opening our eyes to the water we need for soul refreshment.

## Your Thirst for Better Encouragement

When Gabriela Andersen-Schiess's body stiffened and cramped twenty miles into her 1984 marathon, it wasn't her heart that had grown weary; it was her muscles. Physical dehydration was to blame. With six miles left to go, she'd unintentionally run right past the fifth and final water station. Her body overheated because it lacked adequate hydration and nourishment.

As we run, we must take heed of discouragement as an indicator of spiritual thirst. When Christians require nourishment and refreshment, we need words of truth that fill our soul with the nourishing promise of good that comes from God alone. We need him to spur us on to endurance and victory. We can't overlook the signs meant to lead us in the direction of spiritual hydration.

In Psalm 69, when David was overwhelmed and sinking into a deep mire, he confessed his weariness to God. He acknowledged that his throat felt parched from crying out and his eyes grew dim with waiting. He recognized his fears of the waters overtaking him and his temptation to give up the struggle. David knew he lacked strength and endurance and when he was worried he couldn't wait any longer, he confessed this need to God and watched for God's help and encouragement to come. Nothing was hidden: feelings of loneliness, persecution, shame, dishonor, his lack of comforters, his real and present enemies who'd given him poison for food and sour wine to drink. David wasn't afraid to take stock of how dire his situation felt because he trusted the promises of God. Isaiah 41:17 assures us that God satisfies his children's thirst: "When the poor and needy seek water, and there is none, and their tongue is parched with thirst, I the LORD will answer them; I the God of Israel will not forsake them."

As spiritual runners attempting to "run with endurance the race that is set before us," God expects our desire for help and support. He anticipates your spiritual exhaustion. But he also desires for us to come to him for encouragement first and to return repeatedly. When we believe that God watches over us as we run, looks out for us in our weariness, and desires to provide for our hunger and thirst, we won't feel quite as panicked when our stadium seems emptied of spectators and cheerleaders. We will know how and where to find better encouragement that will cheer us forward with every step. Each and every week inside the gathering of the local church, God's word and God's people serve as water stations of refreshment.

As Jesus met the woman at the well in John 4 he noticed she'd come alone and in need in the middle of the day to fill her empty bucket with well water. Jesus sidesteps pleasantries and offers her more than a listening ear, friendship, or kind words. He offers to ease the more pressing source of her discomfort—her sin. He uncovers her emptiness in order to fill her with the living water that would continually satisfy her. He doesn't encourage her toward moral living in her own strength or renewed self-confidence. He gives her the better news that "whoever drinks of the water" that Christ provides "will never be thirsty again." Later in the story, the woman leaves her water jar and runs into the town to invite the people to come and see Christ. The fruit of better encouragement is a renewed and joyful witness.

Thirsty runners must come and drink. The God of encouragement has prepared a table and invited his people to "come, everyone who thirsts, come to the waters" (Isa. 55:1). In the Gospels, Christ repeats the invitation and clarifies that he, the Messiah, is the living water, and "if anyone thirsts, let him come to me and drink. Whoever believes in me, as the Scripture has said, 'Out of his heart will flow rivers of living water'" (John 7:37–38).

Your heart thirsts for the refreshing good news that's found only through the promises of Christ because the gospel message "speaks a better word" (Heb. 12:24) than anything you have to offer and better than any message the world has to offer you. The God of endurance and encouragement offers his people better encouragement by offering himself. Romans 15:4 invites us to come for lasting hydration, saying, "whatever was written in former days was written for our instruction, that through endurance and through the encouragement of the Scriptures we might have hope."

If you are in Christ, you need his better encouragement. And for the remainder of this book, the outline below will serve as a working definition of the kind of encouragement necessary to sustain Christian faith and endurance. Here's what I want you to remember.

**Better encouragement:**

provides God's promises

to God's people

in order to help us endure

with our hope set on Christ.

Fix your eyes on God's promises and take courage. The God of endurance and encouragement is with you and will satisfy your thirst.

3

# The Substance of Encouragement

ON OUR FAMILY'S FIRST EASTER SUNDAY in Baltimore, the cherry blossom tree in our backyard burst forth with brilliant white celebratory flowers, just in time for our Easter service. The gathering would be small; we arranged dining room chairs on our back deck and soon a few families would gather together to worship, sing hymns, and hear the gospel proclaimed. We prayed our voices and the meditations of our hearts would be like the blossoms and the cool morning breeze, proclaiming the truth of the newness of life.

Because half our attendees were young children, my husband planned a special message for the kids. Borrowing from our own stash of family discipleship resources, he brought out the container marked "Resurrection Eggs" that we purchased from the local Christian bookstore. Over the past decade my husband and I have told the Easter story to our own children every year by using twelve colorful plastic Easter eggs, each filled with a tiny treasure representing a various scriptural element of the Easter story: a coin to symbolize Judas's betrayal, clasped hands for Jesus's prayer in the garden of Gethsemane, a silver cup, a crown of thorns, and a white linen cloth. Year after year, each of our children looks forward to examining and passing around the treasures.

This Easter morning would be the first time some of the children attending our church had heard the gospel or the resurrection story. My husband passed out the twelve eggs and explained how the story would go. As he read each egg's scripture, he would point to the child whose turn it was to reveal what was hidden inside. Then each treasure would be passed around for all to see. At the end everyone would give the toys back. The children listened attentively, each waiting for their turn. One at a time, eleven children opened their eggs. Eleven children discovered the treasure inside and passed the toy around the circle for all to examine. Eleven Bible verses were read aloud.

Finally, it was time for seven-year-old Phoebe to open the twelfth egg. An anxious, anticipatory smile spread across her face. She turned to face the watching crowd. With every eye locked on her, each child assuming we'd saved the best for last, Phoebe couldn't wait to be the one to reveal the amazing gift inside. Her fingers carefully popped open the white egg. But to her horror, the white egg appeared to hold no treasure. "It's *empty?*" she cried incredulously. Then she burst into tears; because she didn't understand the gospel's promises, she didn't realize she'd been given the very best egg, filled with the very best treasure of all.

## Empty Faith

Discouragement attempts to persuade Christians to believe that our faith holds no treasure, the cross is emptied of its power, and we cannot trust God to provide for us. We assume if we've professed faith, we should always feel #blessed. When we do not discern God's tangible provision, we assume he hasn't provided good, riches, or blessing and we behave as though we must squint to catch a glimpse of God's meager provision in our daily life. Because we struggle to see all the good that God has richly provided, we fail to believe all that God has promised, even though we are called to walk by faith and not by sight. And yet, God sees and attends to our weakness by making promises that will continually encourage us when we doubt and convince us that we will "look upon the goodness of the LORD in the land of the living" (Ps. 27:13).

We are often not convinced by God's goodness or provision because he provides differently than we expect and slower than we'd like. When we pause to read Scripture or pray in accordance with God's promises, we expect to see an immediate return on investment. We want microwaveable mercies so that healing happens fast and minute-by-minute miracles so we don't lose focus or faith. But many times, our agenda and timetable are not God's. In Scripture, God's people must often wait for his direction, seek his answers, look for his provision, plead for his rescue, and wait on his healing. Our irritability and discomfort do not sway God to action, nor do they negate his good promises. God still sustains his doubting people as they wait on him; his mercies are new every morning.

We are not trained or skilled in looking for the riches of God's mercies because our culture has trained us to "get it, girl!" by going in search of whatever we want and not settling until we've "believed and received." But what if we haven't learned to treasure what we should or desire what God wants? We are often emptied of our ability to trust God because we are wrongly presuming upon mercies that aren't promised instead of looking to God's promises and trusting he will provide good. While most of us are privileged to live in a society where we feel capable of providing many things for ourselves, we must be cautious not to assume the ability to lay hold of every good blessing or wield all power on our own.

Discouragement regularly startles and unsettles us because it reminds us we aren't in control. When we run out of milk we can hop in the car, drive to the store, and purchase more. But what about when we're out of patience or trust? We are easily frustrated when we cannot ship wisdom, knowledge, power, or the fruit of the Spirit to our front door. We are surprised when life reminds us that even when we choose to be happy, we can't always change our circumstances. When what we want is not within our grasp, when we don't hold all the answers or can't access the resources we'd like, we worry that God hasn't provided what we need. We doubt he's given us *every* good thing.

Tim Keller reasons that few Christians are purely motivated by a sincere desire to seek truth; we can all look back on our lives and observe choices and patterns that reveal a more sinister desire. We want to be in charge. And yet God came after us, found us, graciously helped us see our own blindness, and exposed our unwarranted distrust of him. Keller writes that in order for many of us to notice or admit our own sinful self-interest, desire for control, and inadequate dependence on God, we must be "mugged by reality."[1] When life is simple and easy, we have no reason to feel

1    Timothy Keller, *Hope in Times of Fear: The Resurrection and the Meaning of Easter* (New York: Viking, 2021), 16–17.

our need for God's help. But when we're shaken silly by certain unfavorable circumstances like a sudden breakup, a cross-country move, a difficult pregnancy, or an undiagnosable illness, we're graciously called to pay attention to an existing reality we may not want to notice. The struggle is a necessary part of the process of our sanctification.

## Empty Promises

Initially, we may not expect to experience seasons of doubt or unbelief. The trouble with doubt is that it tries to stay hidden. We can't see our own blind spots. We need help. So God often uses discouragement to uncover our existing doubts that we wouldn't have otherwise noticed or confessed. It's easy to believe we "can do all things in Christ" when the only thing our day requires of us is making our bed or picking up a gallon of milk from the store. But it's harder to believe the same promise when we're actively struggling with self-control, lacking any sign of joy, or unable to climb out of our unforgiveness. How do we cling to promises or reap encouragement from them when we feel painfully unconvinced?

These are the kinds of common doubts and discouragements that tend to appear later in the course of our sanctification as we learn to walk by faith, not early on when it feels new and exciting and the burden of believing is light. In the beginning, we are eager to hear and respond to God's word, zealous for kingdom work, and willing to courageously sacrifice our time and energy. We think, "Lay down our desires to serve others? Okay! Mission field? Sure! Martyrdom? Lord, if it's your will!" But as we march into battle and our feet get bogged down in mud and mire and we experience significant testing of our faith, we are forced to stare many of God's promises in the face and decide for ourselves whether or not we will choose to believe them in adversity and look to Christ when only he can sustain. Doubt feels spiritually draining and we grow weary from fighting to believe.

Tired of trusting, we revert to old worldly patterns; we convince ourselves it feels easier to abide by laws and schedules than it does to rest in grace. Instead of desiring to be shaped and changed into God's likeness, we attempt to control, simplify, and fix in order to sustain ourselves. We know God promises to be with us, but how should this encouragement help us, practically speaking, when it comes to obeying his commands or fleeing temptation and sin?

Doubt often grows from small seeds of unbelief: Is God with me? Can I trust him? Will he provide me with good? Instead of asking God to give us what we need to trust him and walk by faith, we doubt that what the Creator of the universe has told his creatures is trustworthy, good, and true. We are tempted to believe God will let us down just like people often do.

Because we know that we are like leaves shaken with every wind, God has given us his promises to remind us of every good and perfect gift that comes from above and to act as a tangible assurance of his promised good. We have plenty of reasons to believe all of his substantial promises are both good and true and able to fill our hearts with good.

We are often like the twelve spies sent to scope out the promised land—we take a cursory look around but fail to notice the abundant signs of blessing meant to lead us to trust, gratitude, and joy. When we fail to trust God and take encouragement from his promises, our hearts remain discouraged and doubts increase.

We need encouragement that rightly assures us that we do not have all we need on our own and that we cannot help ourselves; we need to "know the love of Christ that surpasses knowledge" in order to be filled with the fullness of God (Eph. 3:19).

### Promise-Filled Encouragement

In the Old Testament, God establishes covenant promises with Israel in order to sustain his people during their slavery, wilderness wandering, rebellion, and uncertainty. These covenant promises become the driving force of God's encouragement to his people: the Abrahamic, Mosaic, and Davidic covenants each act as a compass, pointing Israel back in the direction of God when they are lost or wandering. God's covenants remind Israel what is good, what is true, and how God has called them to live in obedience to him. God makes promises to his people that he plans to fulfill in order to give them a future and a hope, to assure them of his goodness, and to prepare them to call upon his name (Jer. 29:10–12).

Overall, God's covenant promises encourage his people to believe that he is their better provider. First, in the Abrahamic covenant, God promises to make Abraham the father of many nations, with descendants as numerous as the stars. In Genesis 15:5, God declares, "Look toward heaven, and number the stars, if you are able to number them. . . . So shall your offspring be." The Lord had the authority to extend this covenant to an old, unlikely recipient, promising to multiply his children, bless them, and "give this land" to them (Gen. 15:18).

Over the years, God repeatedly reminds and reassures Abraham of this covenant when he is confused, frustrated, and tempted by unbelief. Even when Abraham grows discouraged and attempts to take control of the situation, God isn't strong-armed; but he does encourage him by way of gentle reminder. God affirms his promise by telling Abraham,

> my covenant is with you, and you shall be the father of a multitude of nations. . . . *I will* make you exceedingly fruitful, and *I will* make you into nations, and kings shall come from you. And *I will* establish my covenant between me and you and your offspring after you throughout their generations for an everlasting covenant, to be God to you and to your offspring after you. (Gen. 17:4, 6–7)

God encourages Abraham by assuaging his doubts with the assurance of his promises.

Then, through the Mosaic covenant, God promises to deliver Moses and the Israelite people from slavery and captivity to a good land. God's covenant is repeatedly the word of encouragement given to Israel as they groan and cry to him for help and deliverance (Ex. 2:23–24). God hears and answers, promising,

> *I am the* Lord, and *I will bring you out* from under the burdens of the Egyptians, and *I will deliver you* from slavery to them, and *I will redeem you* with an outstretched arm and with great acts of judgment. *I will take you to be my people*, and *I will be your God*, and you shall know that *I am the* Lord *your God*, who has brought you out from under the burdens of the Egyptians. *I will bring you into the land that I swore to give* to Abraham, to Isaac, and to Jacob. *I will give it to you* for a possession. *I am the* Lord. (Ex. 6:6–8)

Finally, in the Davidic covenant, God assures Israel as they yearn for their own king to rule over their land that he will appoint one of their descendants to sit on the throne and reign forever. In this promise, they hear, "God will give us," "God will make us," "We will be great." But again, the Lord's covenant doesn't center around the glory of the recipients; he has a better King and better kingdom in mind in 1 Chronicles 17:1–11 when he promises to make a name for David "like the name of the great ones of the earth" and to appoint a place for his people where he will plant them and they will dwell securely in their own land. God will subdue their enemies, build a house, and raise up David's offspring as he establishes his kingdom, and David's descendant will sit on the throne, reigning over Israel forever. God does not encourage Israel by the word of his covenant promise in order to make Israel self-confident, socially impressive, or politically powerful; he encourages them so they'd look with anticipation for a coming King.

Thus, God makes promises to his people in order to clearly declare his good intentions, remind them of his presence and provision, and encourage them to trust that he will carry out his plans throughout all of creation. In each of these covenants, God encourages his people in order to prepare them to wait and watch for his better provision until it comes in full.

## Covenant-Keeping Encouragement

In the Old Testament, God's covenants were conditionally based on the people's obedience: God would fulfill his promises to his people if his people loved and obeyed him perfectly. Though these are conditions we're used to, this is not the way we want our righteousness determined for eternity since "all have sinned and fall short of the glory of God" (Rom. 3:23).

We don't want our righteousness based on the word "if" when the condition depends on our good behavior—when we're only rewarded *if* we love God, *if* we keep his commandments, *if* we are careful to do all that is contained in God's law, *if* we do not fear, and *if* we stand firm through the end. If. If. If. If we're honest, this system wouldn't end well for us. If we were in charge of earning our righteousness, we would have nothing good: no good promises, no good reward, no hope of redemption.

For 430 years after God made his covenant promise to Abraham, God's people lived under the guardianship of the law because of their transgressions; they wrestled under the burden of their unrighteousness, imprisoned by sin and held captive by the desires of their hearts. And even after four centuries' worth of God's people coming face to face with their own sin, insufficiency, and doubt—being, as Keller put it, "mugged" by the reality of their idolatry and unbelief—not one of them could perfectly keep the law.[2] We can't either. We all require a better covenant that doesn't depend on our perfection or goodness.

Broken, fallen, sinful idolaters like you and me need a covenant that does not depend on our own covenant-keeping ability but on Christ's perfection. Because we cannot wholly keep the law and will not flawlessly abide by God's rigorous sacrificial system or perfectly atone for every sin, we need Christ to do it—to do what we cannot do for ourselves. When the law of God judges our heart and finds us wanting, we won't need af-

2    Keller, *Hope in Times of Fear*, 16–17.

firmation or compliments to stand firm at the judgment seat. In the final day, sinners will need the assurance of God's pardon, granted only through the intercession of his Son. As we await the final day, our greatest source of confidence and courage comes from the covenant of grace; we are recipients of an inheritance we did not earn.

Only when we understand our own weakness and insufficiency will we rejoice in the good news that God desires "mercy, . . . not sacrifice" (Matt. 9:13) and find freedom in the reality that "now that faith has come, we are no longer under a guardian, for in Christ Jesus you are all sons of God, through faith. . . . if you are Christ's, then you are Abraham's offspring, heirs according to promise" (Gal. 3:25–26, 29). Through the good news of the gospel, you've been freed from the conditional clause of your own good behavior.

God has provided a new covenant with new terms and conditions: if God's people, who are called by his name, will humble themselves, trusting and believing in the powerful forgiveness and redemption found only through the cross and the resurrection of Jesus, then God will hear and save. Your sins will be forgiven through the better covenant of grace, through the blood of Christ. God encouraged you to trust him by establishing his covenant and then sending his perfect Son to confirm his oath to a wandering, doubting people.

Hebrews 6:17–18 says that because "God desired to show more convincingly to the heirs of the promise the unchangeable character of his purpose," he guaranteed his covenant with an oath, so that by these two unchangeable things, "in which it is impossible for God to lie, we who have fled for refuge might have strong encouragement to hold fast to the hope set before us." God sent Christ as our firstfruit, assuring us to take courage in his ability to save and redeem.

The God of endurance and encouragement provided Christ's resurrection as an early taste of the coming redemption in order to better show his truthfulness and confirm the promises given to the patriarchs so that you would glorify him for his mercy (Rom. 15:8–9). You can trust God's word will prove true, because it was by his command that the Word became flesh and dwelt among us. The covenant of grace "speaks a better word than the blood of Abel" (Heb. 12:24) and is a better encouragement because it guarantees access to

- **A better assurance** that belongs to salvation (Heb. 6:9)
- **A better hope** by which you may draw near to God (Heb. 7:19)
- **A better covenant** through Jesus (Heb. 7:22), enacted on **better promises** of grace (Heb. 8:6)
- **A better possession**, abiding inheritance, and reward (Heb. 10:34), **a better country**, and **better life** in heaven (Heb. 11:16, 35)

You will be better encouraged to endure when your hope is fixed on the promises of your covenant-keeping God whose love is better than life (Ps. 63:3).

## The Substance of Better Encouragement

Christians are often tempted to believe that if they experienced the presence of God like Abraham, Moses, and David, their faith would be strong too. But these men died before receiving what God had promised. Friend, Hebrews 11:39–40 tells us that we have a better vantage point from which to view our inheritance with the saints. We are able to glimpse and be encouraged by the promised covenant and the fulfillment of Christ in a way that Abraham, Moses, and David weren't able to imagine. And yet, thousands of years later, we all wait eagerly together by the hope of the very same good promise.

As you and I continue to reap the benefits of God's word—reading, reminding our hearts of our source of hope, and repeating God's promises to one another—we must be cautious not to manipulate God's promises into words of encouragement that the Spirit hasn't intended. The word must speak pointedly as a sword of truth, not as a magic wand to grant wishes.

We are prone to see the Abrahamic covenant as God's promise to provide Abraham and Sarah with a baby and then assume God will grant us a baby too. When we apply God's promises in this way, we behave as though we know God's will for our lives and that we are responsible for feeling our way forward in the dark. But God never asked us to solve our own problems, impress him with our creativity or resourcefulness, or dig ourselves out of trouble with our own self-help solutions. When we believe that we must work to earn God's blessing or approval, discouragement is sure to follow. God's promise to Abraham was not meant to be satisfied through the opening of any praying woman's womb. God already fulfilled his promise to Abraham long ago on Calvary when through Christ's death he granted new life to all those who would believe in him. So while God does not open every womb, he's done something extraordinarily better—he's opened a way for new birth so that you could be grafted into his family, accepted as his child, and encouraged through the sacrifice of his Son.

Similarly, the Mosaic covenant was not God's promise to fully deliver you from slavery to food, alcohol, or shopping. He might, or you might struggle as long as you live on this broken earth. But because Christ already fulfilled the Mosaic covenant promise, you can trust he will one day present you blameless, free from the chains of your sin and slavery. Christ anchors you to this new covenant promise and encourages you to await the better land where you will enjoy eternal freedom. And last, the Davidic covenant doesn't promise us victory or fame here. But through Christ, we are joined to all the people of God through the new covenant of grace and encouraged by our citizenship in a heavenly kingdom where we will be joint heirs with Christ.

Today, God encourages his people in order to prepare us to wait and watch for Christ's return when he will fully usher in his better provision in the new kingdom to come. As you wait for Christ's return with a longing for strength and endurance, consider this exhortation from author Jon Bloom:

> Jesus does not want us to be discouraged. In fact, he commands us not to be. Listen to what Jesus says to his disciples just before what probably was the most discouraging experience of their lives—his brutal death: "Let not your hearts be troubled" (John 14:1). Christians need encouragement that is filled with the promises of God—or "faith-fueled courage"—particularly when their faith feels choked by discouragement.[3]

3   Jon Bloom, "Don't Let Discouragement Choke You," *Desiring God*, August 24, 2012, https://www.desiringgod.org/.

Reap the rich rewards of the covenant of grace by applying the promised encouragement as it was meant to be. Christ's divine power has granted to you "all things that pertain to life and godliness, through the knowledge of him" as well as "his precious and very great promises" so that you might partake of the divine nature (2 Pet. 1:3, 4) that fills your heart with his wisdom and understanding, his mercy and grace, his power, his strength, his comfort, and his ability to sustain you by his word.

## Because the Tomb Is Empty, You Are Not

On our fifth Easter in Baltimore, several new church friends gathered around the dining room table. As we ate, my teenage daughter told the story of poor Phoebe's Easter devastation. As our friends laughed about the misunderstanding, I thought about how each woman gathered around the table had experienced her own share of heartache or devastation that year. And in the midst of our pain, we hadn't laughed about the surprise and hurt we'd each felt in our own trials as our faith had been tested. Discouragement had tempted each of us to question God's good promises while we waited to feel the comfort of the cross.

Around the table were women who'd learned to trust that God's word always proves true. In times of darkness, God's covenant of grace was a shield about us—equipping me in the weariness of homeschooling during a pandemic, defending the hope of two mothers whose pregnancies recently ended in miscarriage, fighting the fears of a child with learning disabilities, protecting the joy of an aging saint who suffers from dementia, and strengthening her daughter to continue to stand firm as she cares for her mother. Each of us knew our daily need for God's encouragement; each found mercy in Christ who was bruised for our transgressions.

Because Jesus laid down his life and was raised to new life, we'd been filled by his Spirit. We had all the encouragement we needed to endure our own difficulties, continuing to lay down our lives while obediently following him toward hope. We could walk by faith with joy in the thought of the coming resurrection, even when daily life felt disappointing. God will continue to encourage, sustain, and tenderly carry each of us through the wilderness as Christ nourishes our souls with his living water. As we abide by the help of the Spirit, he will adorn our lives with the budding blossoms of spiritual fruit that burst in celebratory praise to the Creator.

Christ's resurrection fills the Christian's life and faith with the promise of his abundant riches. We are the recipients of a better, fuller, sweeter, more substantial encouragement. Because of Jesus, we are encouraged "to reach all the riches of full assurance of understanding and the knowledge of God's mystery" that is in him, where God has "hidden all the treasures of wisdom and knowledge" (Col. 2:2–3).

# 4

# The Power of Encouragement

IN 1952 NORMAN VINCENT PEALE published his wildly popular self-help book, *The Power of Positive Thinking*.[1] Because Peale's thoughts have circulated throughout our culture for seventy years, many of our hearts have been marinated and tenderized by his principles and others that sound similar, even if we aren't familiar with his teachings or haven't personally read the book.

In Peale's first chapter, "Believe in Yourself," he offers readers a list of "workable rules for overcoming inadequacy attitudes and learning to practice faith."[2] By practicing what Peale preaches, he promises you will "build up confidence" and have a "new feeling of power."[3] For the sake of brevity, I've summarized the list of ten exhortations below:

---

1  Norman Vincent Peale, *The Power of Positive Thinking* (New York: Touchstone, 2015).
2  Peale, *Power of Positive Thinking*, 12–13.
3  Peale, *Power of Positive Thinking*, 12–13.

1. Never accept failure; tenaciously focus on succeeding.
2. Silence negative thoughts by canceling them out with positive thoughts.
3. Don't fixate on obstacles; study and eliminate them.
4. Don't be awestruck by other people; you do you.
5. Ten times a day, slowly and confidently repeat Romans 8:31, "If God be for us, who can be against us?"
6. Get a counselor to help you uncover your inferiority issues and self-doubt that likely began in childhood.
7. Ten times a day, affirm yourself by speaking the "magic statement" of Philippians 4:13 out loud: "I can do all things through Christ which strengtheneth me."
8. Estimate your own ability and then raise it by ten percent; believe in "your own God-released powers."
9. Put yourself in God's hands by telling yourself you are, believing it, and then affirming that "the kingdom of God is within you."
10. Remind yourself God is with you, nothing can defeat you, and that you receive power from him.[4]

Peale's book became so popular that it remained on the *New York Times* bestsellers list for 186 weeks and sold 2.5 million copies in just 4 years. By 1993 the book had sold more than 15 million copies, was widely recognized as one of the nation's bestselling nonfiction books of all time, and had been translated into over 40 languages.[5] Peale's rules catechized society at large because his

---

4  Peale, *Power of Positive Thinking*, 12–13.
5  Russell Chandler, "Norman Vincent Peale, 'Minister to Millions,' Dies: Religion: Mixing Faith and Psychology, Author of 'The Power of Positive Thinking' Spread

power of positivity promised others the power to feel better, do better, act better, believe better, and make life better.

Because readers liked the illusion of power, they were willing to overlook the negative critiques from biblical scholars, psychologists, and medical professionals who warned that Peale's instructions weren't helpful, biblical, or good. Peale attempted to encourage Christians with worldly wisdom, a little pop psychology, and a handful of Bible verses sprinkled in for good measure. Only a few of the principles were legitimately helpful: working with a counselor, filling one's mind with Scripture, and affirming one's belief in God's power. But on the whole, the majority of the solutions weren't filled with the power of the gospel or even basic biblical wisdom. Instead, it sounded like the world.

The concept of never accepting failure stood in direct opposition to Romans 6:11 that encouraged believers to "consider yourselves dead to sin and alive to God in Christ Jesus." And was Peale suggesting that sinners struggling under the weight of conviction should not fixate on obstacles when confronted on matters of sin and instead simply focus on the positive? Weren't Christians supposed to be encouraged to flee sin, not chase it with a spoonful of sugar? Even the two rules that suggested repeating specific scriptures ten times a day seemed to suggest that the power behind the word came not from the Spirit but from humanity's legalistic discipline.

## Rebranding the Power of Positivity

As a young mom, I often longed for encouragement because I felt utterly powerless. I felt powerless when it came to being

Inspiration Worldwide," *Los Angeles Times*, December 26, 1993, https://www.la times.com/.

a gentle and engaged mother while still keeping up with dirty dishes, laundry, groceries, and other household responsibilities. I felt powerless in soothing and calming a screaming baby with reflux. I felt powerless to grow in the desire to pray or read my Bible more regularly. Frankly, I felt powerless to please God. In those moments, I desired encouragement that would empower me to face all the battles raging inside my heart and engage them with confidence.

In my earliest days of parenting, women were just beginning to seek and find encouragement within the digital world of mommy blogs. The internet made it easy to connect with plenty of other discouraged women who felt as equally powerless as I did. Depending on the community, I was sometimes empowered by encouragement that served as iron sharpening iron, while at other times, the words merely coddled me in my sin by providing a space where misery loved company.

Journalist Ruth S. Barrett first stumbled upon a mommy blog back in 2013 right after her husband accepted a demanding new job and she felt "constantly irritable and hard-pressed to find any joy in life."[6] At the time, she admits she was coping with her discouragement by doing a lot of yelling. So when a friend emailed her one of Glennon Doyle's viral blog posts, Barrett felt desperate enough for encouragement that she clicked and read, despite her urge to overlook what she assumed would be more "yawnable platitudes."[7]

---

6 Ruth S. Barrett, "The Gospel According to Glennon: How Christian Blogger Glennon Doyle Melton Blew Up My Life and She Knew It and Became the Guru of the Moment," *ELLE*, May 24, 2017, https://www.elle.com/.

7 Barrett, "The Gospel According to Glennon."

As she read, she was encouraged. Doyle's writing felt like "a cri de coeur against the extreme cost of motherhood and its capacity to erode the self."[8] Barrett, like millions of other women, "got hooked on [Doyle's] drip-feed of juicy confessions" and found her "suburban battle hymns fortifying" even though she was Jewish and had different religious beliefs.[9] Repeating Doyle's mantras to herself throughout the day—"I can do hard things," "I am not afraid," "I was born to do this"—empowered and encouraged her all the same.[10]

Doyle's message of encouragement was for the Jew and the Gentile. It had positively empowered Barrett to endure the slings and arrows of motherhood as she cleaned up her child's fruit-snack puke. But the encouragement that Doyle used to empower Barrett wasn't the better encouragement meant to uniquely encourage Christian women. It wasn't the gospel of Jesus. It was preaching the power of positivity that fuels women for a life of self-empowerment.

## Why Does God Empower?

People feel powerless, often because they are. In order for God's people to persevere in periods where powerlessness felt especially painful, they needed the encouragement and assurance of God's power at work on their behalf. For example, in the book of Judges the Israelites began to obey God's command to go into the promised land, devote all their enemies to destruction, and take possession of the land. This task seemed immense and challenging even

8  Barrett, "The Gospel According to Glennon."
9  Barrett, "The Gospel According to Glennon."
10  Barrett, "The Gospel According to Glennon."

though God had already promised them victory, so they needed to be encouraged to obey God and complete the work set before them. To achieve victory, God required his people to faithfully go into battle and fight the terrifying enemies in the land.

One enemy town, Kiriath-sepher, had been particularly challenging to conquer and Israel had become either too afraid or too apathetic to go in and defeat the enemy. So Caleb, the leader of the tribe of Judah, stirred Israel back to work by incentivizing them with a battle prize. Whichever warrior successfully rallied the troops and defeated the enemy would be awarded a bride and a dowry as a thank-you gift from Caleb. God blessed Caleb's motivational tactics and a young warrior named Othniel rose to the task and succeeded in conquering the land.

Even though we tend to shudder at the thought of an arranged marriage in our current culture, this story was likely a win-win situation that fulfilled God's commands and, in the process, blessed every involved party. God blessed Caleb by sending a skilled warrior. God judged Kirath-sepher's wicked idolatry and provided Israel with the land of their inheritance. God blessed Achsah with a skilled warrior as a husband and blessed Othniel with a victory, a bride, and a land.

But in Judges 1:14–15, Achsah asked for more; she urged her new husband Othniel to also request a field from her father. When Caleb saw his daughter, he asked her, "What do you want?" and she responded, "Give me a blessing. Since you have set me in the land of the Negeb, give me also springs of water." The Negeb was a land that was parched and barren; Achsah's dowry was a dry, mountainous land that wasn't suitable for farming. And the couple would be too far away from drinkable water, unable to grow crops, and unable to feed and water their livestock. They needed her father to bless them with a sustainable source of water.

In response, "Caleb gave her the upper springs and the lower springs" (Judg. 1:15). When Achsah's father blessed the couple, he gave them land ownership that assured them the right to continuously abide in peace by the streams of abundance. In the safety of their own land, fruit trees could grow, their leaves would not fail, and the happy couple could feast on food by the banks of the river (Ezek. 47:12). Just like Caleb empowered Othniel and Achsah, so does God empower his people today—by meeting physical needs, extending the blessing of sonship, and fostering nourishment, growth, and rest in the lives of those he loves.

God's promises are able to encourage his children today because they powerfully testify to the Father's desire and ability to understand our needs and graciously give us a blessing too. Because God has met our greatest need for a Savior through the gospel of Jesus, he now welcomes us as his children, and he will pour out his blessing in order to provide the living water we need to be planted by streams of water, remain rooted in fertile soil, grow, mature, produce spiritual fruit, labor in the harvest, and abide in peace.

### Empowered by God's Blessing

In Judges 3:12, the land of Israel was polluted by idolatrous enemies and "the people of Israel again did what was evil in the sight of the LORD." Forgetting God's merciful deliverance from slavery and their promised inheritance, they forgot God, served the idols of the land, and kindled the anger of the Lord. As a sign of judgment, God sold his children into the hand of their enemies, where they would labor in the anguish of slavery for eight long years. When Israel finally cried out to the Lord for deliverance, he raised up Othniel as a deliverer for the people of Israel. And the Spirit of the Lord was upon Othniel to judge Israel, to go out to war, to prevail over Israel's enemies, and to deliver the land of Israel to forty years of rest (Judg. 3:9).

God did not allow Israel's wicked idolatry to continue indefinitely. Israel's boundary crossing and rule breaking eventually caught up to them. God's anger was stirred, his judgment handed down, and the people were enslaved. Idolatrous Israel had no power to escape their punishment with God as the enforcer. The people had no power of their own. After eight years of slavery, they finally caved, admitted to their sin and powerlessness, and plead with God for rescue. In an act of great compassion, God sent a deliverer to rescue his people from slavery.

God's Spirit empowered Othniel to serve as a judge, even though he was just an average man. God called Othniel to labor for the good of his rebellious people under extreme opposition and difficulty not because of his innate leadership skills or likability among the people but because this was God's sovereign plan of deliverance. In the Hebrew language the name Othniel means "force of God"[11] and commentators often interpret the name to imply that he was a "lion of God,"[12] sent to serve as a prophetic symbol of Israel's coming deliverance. When Israel's sin enslaved them and they cried out for rescue, God sent Othniel to judge and deliver the pride of Israel, to win a bride, gain an inheritance, and secure rest for the land.

---

11  *Blue Letter Bible*, "עׇתְנִיאֵל," accessed November 19, 2021, https://www.blueletterbible.org/.

12  *Bible Study Tools*, "Othniel," accessed November 19, 2021, https://www.biblestudytools.com/.

But Othniel's story also paints a poetically prophetic portrait of Trinitarian encouragement that should empower the broken and wandering hearts of Christians today. Even though we wrestle in our flesh against the same idolatry and sin, God has promised that a greater deliverer, a more powerful lion, is yet to come. When the true Lion of Judah comes to earth to judge, save, and deliver his people, he will fight more forcefully and conquer more fully than Othniel did. When Christ comes in power he will win his bride and gather his people as his inheritance, and instead of the slavery we deserve, we will rule and reign with the Lion of Judah who sits enthroned on high. Othniel's story is a blessing and an encouragement to Christians because it relieves us from the belief that we can fully save or deliver ourselves. Our deliverance is always an unfathomable blessing provided by God.

## Empowered by Christ

The God of encouragement and endurance extends the blessing of his power in order to help his people, not fill them with greater self-sufficiency. In the Old Testament, God's Spirit was poured out in order to corporately guide and sustain the hearts of all of the Israelite people and to empower leaders (like Noah, Abraham, Moses, and Joshua), speak through prophets (like Isaiah and Ezekiel), and appoint judges and kings. But just like faithless Israel, we've always wanted more—we long for God with us. And God heard and answered our cry. As recorded in John 1:14, the Word became flesh and dwelt among us and the Father "anointed Jesus of Nazareth with the Holy Spirit and with power" (Acts 10:38) in order to proclaim good news, liberty, and the year of the Lord's favor (Luke 4:18–19).

Throughout Jesus's ministry on earth, each miraculous sign and wonder consistently displayed the love and power of God in order to call sinners to repentance and new life. The Spirit's power enabled Christ to seek and save the lost, heal wounds, bind up demons, and perform numerous public miracles observed by massive crowds of people and well-documented by eyewitnesses. The demonstration of God's power always serves as a gift to many. In Luke 18:35–43, when Jesus drew near to Jericho he encountered a blind man sitting on the roadside who believed in his power to heal. Powerless, the blind man cried out in desperation, pleading for mercy he knew could only come from Christ. The surrounding crowd rebuked and tried to silence the sufferer but he "cried out all the more, 'Son of David, have mercy on me!'" (18:39). Jesus called the man near and asked, "What do you want me to do for you?" (18:41).

The blind man wasn't shy. He didn't try to impress Jesus with a cheerful attitude in suffering or convince him to heal him. He simply told Jesus what he wanted from him: "'Lord, let me recover my sight.' And Jesus said to him, 'Recover your sight; your faith has made you well.' And immediately the man recovered his sight and followed him, glorifying God" (18:41–43). God's power transformed the man and those who gathered around him. When God displays his power, he often does so either to encourage the faith of his children or to prod unbelieving sinners to repent and have faith.

### Empowered by God's Spirit

Jesus prepared his disciples for the dark days after his death by encouraging their patient faithfulness with the promise of a coming Helper. God would baptize his people with his Spirit (Matt.

3:11), fill their hearts with the indwelling power of Christ, and guide them into all truth (John 16:13) *after* Jesus went away. Even though they couldn't see Jesus, God would still lead and empower them for his work, providing the Spirit as his better provision. After Christ's death and resurrection, after Jesus appeared to the apostles, and after they'd waited "for the promise of the Father" (Acts 1:4), the day of Pentecost arrived and the Holy Spirit was poured out on Christ's followers (2:1–12).

When the Spirit descended, the men began to speak in various languages, "devout men from every nation under heaven" were drawn together (2:5), and "visitors from Rome, both Jews and proselytes, Cretans and Arabians" understood the mighty works of God (2:8, 11–12). As the Spirit opened men's eyes to the power and work of God, the prophecy of Joel 2:28–32 was fulfilled. God poured out his Spirit on all flesh, showed himself in signs and wonders, and demonstrated his power to save everyone who calls on the name of the Lord. Because God poured out his Spirit on his people, his children are now filled in lasting measure by his power. The Holy Spirit's power not only opens spiritual eyes and reveals God's truth, it also empowers Christ's disciples to love and obey Jesus and work for his kingdom and glory.

Christ's birth fulfilled the promises of the old covenant of God's law and served as a final oath and testimony to God's faithful, covenant-keeping power, and at Pentecost God proved himself again. By pouring out his Spirit on all flesh, Christ guaranteed the covenant of his mercy and gave his power to all who would believe. Thus, the promise of Christ's gospel and the oath of the Holy Spirit encourages believers to rest in the power of God who works and wills within the hearts of his people.

## What Do You Want?

Decades have passed since Norman Vincent Peale's book was published. But make no mistake, the putrid aroma of self-empowered encouragement still lingers strongly in the air. Today, discouraged women look for positive and empowering encouragement from authors like Glennon Doyle, who has said God called her to write to "make people feel better about their insides" by showing them hers.[13]

*Untamed*, Doyle's most recent book, hit the shelves in 2020 and sold a million copies in the first twenty weeks.[14] Why were women so quick to drink in the encouragement of someone who often referred to herself as a clinically depressed motivational speaker? Had her honesty and authenticity convinced discouraged readers that if she had found power, they could too?

Doyle explained how a trip to the zoo with her children helped her make sense of her life, why it felt off, and what she could do about her restless frustration. As she watched a female cheetah chasing a dirty stuffed bunny tied behind a truck in order to entertain sweaty children so she could win a steak, Doyle realized how much she had in common with the domesticated jungle cat named Tabitha: they were both sad, tamed, and powerless. Doyle decided to reclaim her own sense of power and began by examining every captor in order to untame herself.

Nothing was off limits—faith, friendships, family, all were vulnerable to scrutiny. In the end, she pointed the finger of blame

---

13  Ariel Levy, "Glennon Doyle's Honesty Gospel," *The New Yorker*, February 5, 2021, https://www.newyorker.com/.

14  Wikipedia, s.v. "Untamed," last modified October 24, 2021, 00:34, https://en .wikipedia.org/.

on cultural, societal, and religious expectations that had unwittingly domesticated her. Then, in a mighty display of personal empowerment, she worked to break free of every cage she no longer wished to feel confined by. Doyle delivered herself to a better life. By redefining all that was good and true and breaking free of all unpalatable expectation, she'd found personal freedom and "a new marriage, a new faith, a new worldview, a new purpose, a new family, and a new identity by design instead of default."[15] Now, she was eager to encourage other women to do the same by empowering them to behave like a cheetah.

Of course Doyle felt empowered and free. Like the Israelites who forgot God and went after idols, she'd abandoned all restriction and fully given herself over to self-indulgence and idolatry. Scripture tells Christians that no discipline seems pleasant in the moment. When God's grace suppresses our extravagant and licentious longings and pursuits, the flesh boils because of our disdain for being confined.[16] But whether or not Doyle enjoys obedience to the law, God still requires it and holds his people accountable for sin; he will punish the wicked and unrepentant and those whose lives do not demonstrate the fruit of repentance. When a person comes to faith in Christ, the Spirit empowers them to lay down selfish desires, pick up their cross, and follow him.

Consider the obedience of Jesus, the Lion of Judah, who in the days of his flesh, "offered up prayers and supplications, with loud cries and tears, to him who was able to save him from death, and he was heard because of his reverence" (Heb. 5:7). Because Jesus

---

15  Glennon Doyle, extract from *Untamed* (London: Vermillion, 2020), https://www .penguin.com.au/.

16  Richard Sibbes, *The Bruised Reed* (Edinburgh: Banner of Truth Trust, 2018), 49.

learned obedience through what he suffered in order to be made perfect and secure your salvation, he is qualified to encourage you by the power of his Spirit when you struggle in the flesh. If you've been enslaved to righteousness, rejoice in the encouragement of the Spirit's presence. Though you are constrained by the Spirit, powerless to know what will happen, the Holy Spirit will testify to his power everywhere you go (Acts 20:22–23). What more could you want?

## Encouraged by His Power

If you are a follower of Jesus, you have the power to walk away from worldly messages of self-empowerment that were never intended to encourage God's people. Confess any existing worldly desires for self-empowerment to him and ask the Spirit to encourage you by his words of better promise. You need regular encouragement that preaches the power of Christ over your salvation and your sanctification. You don't need to depend on your own positive thinking because the Spirit is renewing your heart and teaching you to have the mind of Christ. You don't need to feel powerful because you are better led by the Spirit's power.

You can either be empowered to be a servant of Christ or a #girlboss. You can live in the light of God's truth, or you can live your truth. You can be enslaved to Christ or break free from the cages of expectation to run free like a cheetah. Christ does not empower you to be the queen of the jungle and rule over your own kingdom. You are encouraged and empowered by the Spirit of God so that your life will point others to the power of the cross. Bring your heart to his holy resolutions and set yourself "upon that which is good, and against that which is ill . . . with this encouragement, that Christ's grace and power will go along with [you]."[17]

Walk by the power of the Spirit and "you will not gratify the desires of the flesh" (Gal. 5:16). Ask the Lord to empower your words and your speech to be a "demonstration of the Spirit and of power, so that your faith might not rest in the wisdom of men but in the power of God" (1 Cor. 2:4–5). Christian, through the power of the Holy Spirit, you have better encouragement. The God of encouragement provides you with his promises, secured for you by Christ, in order to empower your heart by his Spirit.

17  Sibbes, *Bruised Reed*, 127.

# 5

# The Strength of Encouragement

ON THE LITTLE ISLAND OF GALVESTON, TEXAS, the morning of September 8, 1900 began with cloudy skies and the potential for rain. At that time, the economy and population were booming for the "Jewel of Texas" and the port city seemed poised to become one of Texas' major cities.[1] Some had even nicknamed it the "New York of the West" because it burst with jobs, opportunity, and wealth. But as the day progressed, the skies grew darker, the sea raged, and it looked as though a much larger storm would roll through.

Galveston had been caught off guard by a hurricane that would change the island and countless lives forever. As winds quickened and violent waves crashed over the shores, the residents weren't prepared for the storm to surround and fully engulf the entire island. The storm raged from midday into the pitch-black night, submerging the city 15 feet below sea level. Homes and brick

---

1   Mary G. Ramos, "Galveston's Response to the Hurricane of 1900," *Texas Almanac,* last updated August 2021, https://texasalmanac.com/.

buildings were knocked from their foundations and reduced to rubble. Seven hours after landfall, the 135 miles-per-hour winds had destroyed over 3,600 buildings, rendered 30,000 residents homeless, and killed the remaining 6,000 to 12,000. The Galveston Hurricane of 1900 is the nation's deadliest natural disaster on record.

Why had no one prepared or evacuated? Scientists were able to predict oceanic patterns from observing past storms. One professor of atmospheric science noted that "any modestly educated weather forecaster" would have known that when the hurricane passed north of Cuba, it was headed to the Gulf of Mexico.[2] A breakdown in communication was later traced to the United States' fledgling Weather Bureau in Washington, who'd told Galveston that the hurricane had already passed over Florida and wouldn't be headed their way. The city of Galveston lay in ruins, but no one outside the island would know for two more days.

In the following months, many survivors moved away from the island. When the hurricane's strength exposed man's vulnerability, standing firm and fighting to rebuild seemed too costly. Galveston's economy would never fully bounce back or become the "New York of the West." Today, Galveston is a beach town. And when a strong hurricane approaches, its residents usually evacuate inland and take shelter on higher ground.

## Tempted to Self-Strengthen

In a world that encourages us to strengthen ourselves, hurricanes and other natural disasters have a way of putting humanity's

2  Becky Little, "How the Galveston Hurricane of 1900 Became the Deadliest U.S. Natural Disaster," *History*, August 29, 2017, https://www.history.com/.

lack of strength in perspective. Today, it can be easier to predict the weather than to pay attention to the impending storms that brew inside our hearts. We're often too busy to pay attention to many of our own troublesome feelings, negative experiences, difficult responsibilities, or strained relationships until a giant storm catches us unprepared and we scramble to strengthen ourselves. Unexpected storms tend to knock us down and leave us feeling vulnerable and exposed. When circumstantial winds and waves forcefully pull our heads beneath the water, we shouldn't attempt to save ourselves by our own strength.

In Isaiah 11:12, God offers a powerful storm warning to all humankind, preparing them for what's to come: "He will raise a signal for the nations and will assemble the banished of Israel, and gather the dispersed of Judah from the four corners of the earth." And when the Lord gathers his people, he will "strike down the waves of the sea" of Egypt (Zech. 10:11) and wave his hand over the wind with his scorching breath, destroying it in judgment (Isa. 11:15). God mercifully prepares his people to take shelter from his coming wrath.

When the Lord calls out to the people, he invites them to respond to his warning, saying, "Listen to me in silence, O coastlands; let the peoples renew their strength; let them approach . . . let us together draw near for judgment" (Isa. 41:1). The people on the earth below respond in one of two ways: either as God's people, who draw near to God, or as God's enemies, turning away from him and attempting to strengthen themselves.

The coastland idolaters prepare for the coming storm of God's judgment by banding together like modern-day South Texans anticipating a destructive category-five summer hurricane. Isaiah

41:6–7 says, "Everyone helps his neighbor and says to his brother, 'Be strong!' The craftsman strengthens the goldsmith, and he who smooths with the hammer him who strikes the anvil, saying of the soldering, 'It is good'; and they strengthen it with nails so that it cannot be moved." Rather than heeding the early warning meant to deliver them from the storm of judgement to come, they get to work helping each other tie their idols down like they're trampolines that the God of Israel might blow away in the wind. The people find their strength in numbers; working together, they harden their own resolve, batten down the hatches, and expect to stick around through the storm.

Christians are often tempted to respond to their weakness, sin, or idolatry just like the coastland idolaters. Rather than drawing near to God, repenting of our sin, and renewing our strength in the Lord, we attempt to figure our problems out on our own first. If we can encourage and strengthen ourselves, or find a group of friends who can encourage and strengthen us whenever we are drowning, we prefer to weather the storm our way.

I committed to writing this book just a few months before the COVID-19 pandemic shut down the world. I don't think anyone saw that storm coming. Prepared or not, we all scrambled to make life manageable in a time of chaos. In many ways, life didn't just feel harder—it was legitimately harder. We tried to be strong when the minor inconveniences piled up because we understood the gravity of the situation and the fact that lives were being lost. We tried to be thankful each day because we knew our situation could always be worse. We wanted to honor God and to be strong and courageous, but many of us were too weak and too tired to find the strength on our own.

When the pandemic shut down the world, our lives changed radically and suddenly. We simply weren't prepared to be strong in the ways that were now required. We couldn't strengthen ourselves fast enough. We tried to stay happy and healthy and do our best in the circumstances but many of us were grumpy, depressed, and irritable. The pandemic exposed our vulnerabilities. When weakness wore us down, many women gave up. Some stopped eating healthy food, exercising, or sleeping; others stopped reading their Bible or stopped attending church even when it continued to meet virtually. In tragedy, we either cling to God as our strength and shelter or we drift further away and fail to reach out for his strong arm of rescue.

When we are vulnerable, exposed, and desperate for relief, it is often because we loathe the feeling of frailty and weakness and long to return to feeling on top of the chaos we're comfortable with. We daydream about the way things used to be because we can't yet appreciate the way they are now.

A month before this book was due, I needed rest. After eighteen months of pandemic living, I felt stretched thin from home-schooling and writing and regularly daydreamed about a life without deadlines or responsibilities where I could read a book on a beach somewhere. But that wasn't what God had in store. Instead, I broke my collarbone going down a waterslide, took a trip to the emergency room, and caught COVID. The virus spread one by one through our family of seven and prevented our kids from returning to class on the first day of school. Stuck at home and sitting around with my arm in a sling as I tried to type through the pain wasn't the rest I had in mind. Everything around me seemed to fall apart. The oven broke. The dog scratched her cornea. A child developed a mysterious rash. And we caught a stomach bug. I couldn't make this stuff up. Thankfully, no one dared reach out to say "you got this." It was obvious I didn't. When I feel too weak to be the wife, mom, friend, church member, or writer that God has called me to be, it is good and right for me to recognize my desperation and cry out for the Lord's strength.

## Strengthened to Trust

Turning to God for strength doesn't necessarily look like we think it might. We want to close our eyes, say a prayer, open our eyes, and immediately feel strengthened. More often than not, God strengthens our weak muscles through exercise and ongoing training in righteousness, and we assume this means that God is like a disappointed physical trainer that we've annoyed. But this isn't God's posture toward his children as he works to sanctify. When we do not understand his direction or plan, we can trust that he gently leads the weak.

In Exodus 13:17, after the Israelites were released from slavery, God didn't lead them away from Egypt by taking them on the shortest route: "For God said, 'Lest the people change their minds when they see war and return to Egypt.' But God led the people around by the way of the wilderness toward the Red Sea" (13:18). Even though the land of the Philistines was closer and may have seemed the obvious route, God led his people into the wilderness and straight toward the Red Sea in order to take them on the gentler, more peaceful path to protect them from the terrifying sight of the Philistines and the potential of falling into a battle.

The people didn't fully grasp the kindness and mercy of God's plan. Anyone who was familiar with the land or could read a map would probably have questioned why any leader would suggest a route that took a caravan of 2.4 million men, women, and children and all of their livestock through a desert, straight toward the ocean. No physical training or power of positive thinking could strengthen this group to swim across an ocean or walk their families into a watery grave. And yet, the people followed the guidance of the Lord, led by pillars of cloud and fire, right up to the edge of the ocean, where they would look up just in time to see Pharaoh drawing near with six hundred chariots in pursuit of them.

When Israel feared greatly, they cried out to the Lord and complained to Moses, who responded with this encouragement: "Fear not, stand firm, and see the salvation of the LORD, which he will work for you today. . . . The LORD will fight for you, and you have only to be silent" (Ex. 14:13, 14). When Moses offered these words, God had yet to tell Moses the plan. After Moses encouraged the people to wait for God's rescue, the Lord instructed him to lift up his staff, stretch out his hand over the sea to divide it, and lead the people across on dry ground. Israel's intellectual and physical strength weren't necessary for God's plan to work; God provided for his people by blessing their trust and obedience.

God's strength drove the sea back by a strong east wind, God's strength divided the waters, God's strength held the waters back to form a wall on the people's right and the left, and God's strength led them safely down the narrow path. When the Egyptian enemies pursued, God's strength returned the sea to its normal course, God's strength threw the Egyptians into the midst of the sea, and God's strength covered the chariots and the horses. The Lord's strength saved Israel from slavery and their enemies. And

"Israel saw the great power that the LORD used . . . so the people feared the LORD" and believed in him and his servant Moses (Ex. 14:31).

When you wander in the wilderness and do not understand the route forward, better encouragement reminds you that your strength is not the determining factor. In weakness, God strengthens you to "fear not, stand firm, and see the salvation of the LORD" (Ex. 14:13) so that you will behold God's great power and then fear and believe him.

## An Encouraging Battle Cry

In Deuteronomy 11, after Moses read God's law to the people, he charged them to love God by keeping his charge, statutes, rules, and commandments. Then, Moses encouraged the people again, just as he had when they stood at the foot of the Red Sea, saying,

> Consider the discipline of the LORD . . . his greatness, his mighty hand and his outstretched arm, his signs and his deeds . . . what he did to the army of Egypt . . . how he made the water of the Red Sea flow over them as they pursued after you, and how the LORD has destroyed them to this day, and what he did to you in the wilderness, until you came to this place . . . For your eyes have seen all the great work of the LORD that he did. You shall therefore keep the whole commandment that I command you today, that you may be strong, and go in and take possession of the land that you are going over to possess, and that you may live long in the land that the LORD swore to your fathers to give to them and to their offspring, a land flowing with milk and honey. (11:2–5, 7–9)

Moses encouraged Israel to obey the commands of the Lord because he knew that this was what they needed to do to find their strength in the mighty arm of God. When weariness came, they needed only to remember the numerous visible signs and miracles God had already performed on their behalf and choose to trust his strength and walk forward in obedience. They could trust that God would miraculously bless them with renewed strength.

The call to "be strong and courageous" is a battle cry that's continually spoken to God's people in order to rally them to rise up, prepare for war, and take strength in the God who is "mighty in battle" (Ps. 24:8). The Lord's strong hand led Israel out of Egypt and through the Red Sea, and it would strengthen them in the days to come, through each and every battle (Ex. 13:14).

## Encouraged to Fight for Better Strength

The battle cry that we're familiar with today, "be strong and courageous," was passed down as a means of encouragement from God to Moses, Moses to Joshua, Joshua to Israel, and even later from King David to his son Solomon. But this command was always paired with another equally important exhortation.

Before Moses told Israel to be strong, he instructed them to "keep the whole commandment that I command you today, *that* you may be strong, and go in and take possession of the land that you are going over to possess" (Deut. 11:8). The people's strength was a blessing extended by God as a reward for their obedience. The battle cry called the soldiers to attention, rallying them in unified obedience to God and opposition toward their common enemy.

Eve learned this the hard way. When Satan tempted her to disobey God in Genesis 3, he snuck up on her and acted like a friend who'd simply come to help her out. He convinced her to listen to his lies and empty promises by slowly lowering her guard. Eve didn't appear to see their conversation as a threat; she participated instead of being cautious and restrained. When Satan began casting shadows of doubt over the truth and goodness of God's word and command, she engaged in the conversation, not in an offensive attack. When he made her an offer that sounded better than God's command, she made no effort to resist the idea because she liked the sound of a better blessing, free from cost or consequence. When Eve failed to trust and obey God's word, she was deceived by the serpent and led astray by his lies, and she surrendered the reward of God's protection and blessing. In her defeat, she found the curse.

Similarly, in 2 Kings 18:12, the Assyrian army successfully captured almost all of Judah's fortified cities "because [Judah] did not obey the voice of the LORD their God but transgressed his covenant . . . They neither listened nor obeyed." Partial obedience to God's commands was sinful disobedience; Judah transgressed God's covenant and it led to their inherited cities' capture and a weakened resolve in the face of Assyrian enemies. But the storms of attack didn't stop pounding. The king of Assyria intended to take everything. He set his sights on capturing the remaining city of Jerusalem and sent his messenger, the Rabshakeh, straight to the city gates to encourage Judah's surrender. In 2 Kings 18:19–21, the messenger attempted to intimidate God's people: "On what do you rest this trust of yours? Do you think that mere words are a strategy and power for war? In whom do you now trust, that you have rebelled against me? Behold, you are trusting now in . . . that broken reed of a staff, which will pierce the hand of any man who leans on it."

The Jews had already seen most of their fortified cities conquered by Assyria. It would have been easy to forget that their losses and captivity were the result of the people's disobedience and not the failure of God's strong arm of protection. But when the people were weak and broken down, the Assyrian messenger met them at the city wall with words he pretended would help, save, and bless the people of Judah when God supposedly hadn't.

In reality, the messenger spoke lies in order to intimidate and disunify the people of God so they would be weak in battle. He questioned the leadership of King Hezekiah and his available resources. He mocked the wisdom of the Israelites' trust in God. He slandered the Lord's goodness and strength. And in a predictable final blow, he promised the Jews a better life if they surrendered and made peace with Assyria, claiming that their king, Sennacherib, could provide a better living with more abundant blessing than the simple milk and honey they'd found in the promised land God had given them. If they turned away from God, they could have their own vines, fig trees, drinks of water, and plenty of good land filled with grain, wine, bread, vineyards, olive trees, *and* honey; they would live and not die. Doesn't this all sound familiar?

Satan aims to intimidate and discourage you so that you're too weak and afraid to enter the battle and fight by the strength of God. But the voice of spiritual opposition may not come from a source that looks or sounds scary. Sometimes, the words may sound sweet and sensitive and convince you that the person is on your side. This is how the enemy gets you to drop your guard so that he can disguise and hide his lies inside words you'd never assume were meant to destroy you. Just as you need the encouragement of God's strength to enter the battle in moments of fear and doubt, you also need the encouragement of God's strength during moments of temptation so that you won't give up the battle.

As God's people, we are called to fight the good fight and to "cast off the works of darkness and put on the armor of light" (Rom 13:12). We must "make no provision for the flesh, to gratify its desires" (Rom. 13:14) but be encouraged to "be strong in the Lord and in the strength of his might" (Eph. 6:10). Christian, heed the Lord's warning and respond to his battle cry; put on the whole armor of God, which equips you to "stand against the schemes of the devil" (Eph. 6:11). Better encouragement calls you into battle, rallies you to fight, and guards you from the enemy.

Don't underestimate the presence of your enemy who comes to steal, kill, and destroy. The adversary of your soul actively wars against you, taking aim from every vantage point. When you are unarmed, the enemy will easily drag you off into a battle that you aren't prepared to fight and that you never saw coming. Prepare yourself to stand through the storm, encouraged by the words of strength that assisted Moses, Joshua, Israel, and David. Rise and enter your own spiritual battles, obediently trusting God's Spirit to strengthen you and to crush the enemy like a breaking flood. When you fight the battle, you will see the powerful strength of the Lord. Isaiah 46:8–13 encourages the battle-weary to stand firm by remembering and calling to mind that there is no one like God, that his counsel will stand, and that his salvation will not delay.

## Stand by the Strength of Christ

You can be strong and courageous in the battle against sin and temptation, standing firm in the strength of God, because you've seen Christ perfectly demonstrate full obedience and strength. Christ came in human flesh, clothed in weakness. He had to grow in strength. He had to face temptation in the wilderness and suffer on the cross. Not only can Jesus fully relate to the difficulty of temptation, but he can also fully encourage you to stand firm because he alone proved to be perfectly qualified to do so. When Christ was led into the wilderness by the Spirit in Matthew 4, he showed his followers how to stand firm, encouraged in the strength of God.

After fasting for forty days and nights, our physically exhausted, hungry, and weak Jesus did not bend or break under the enemy's deception. When Satan tempted him, saying, "If you are the Son of God, command these stones to become loaves of bread," Jesus stood firm in the strength of God's word and answered, "It is written, 'Man shall not live by bread alone, but by every word that comes from the mouth of God'" (Matt. 4:3–4). When the devil took him to the pinnacle of the city and later to a very high mountain to tempt him to prove his strength, he stood firm and refused to provide himself with resources or rescue so that the Father might receive all the glory. In trial and temptation, Jesus was encouraged by the Father's will and strengthened by the hope of glory.

Christ's obedience in the wilderness felt like painful discipline at the time, but God would reward his obedience with the blessing of increased strength in his final moments at his crucifixion.

Because Jesus obediently grew in the strength of his Father, he was prepared to stand firm in God's strength even when his body was broken and bruised. Christ did not exercise his authority apart from God or yield up his spirit to death until the will of his Father had been completed (Matt. 27:50). Christ's strength encourages you to stand firm in him; you can cease your anxious toil because his strength brought you near to God by the blood of his sacrifice. Receive the encouragement of Christ's strength in your weakness: "In returning and rest you shall be saved; in quietness and in trust shall be your strength" (Isa. 30:15).

Because Christ did not faint or grow weary, the reproaches of sinful humanity fell on him, and his testimony of victory over the grave renews your strength (Isa. 40:28–29) and enables you to run and not be weary, to walk and not faint (Isa. 40:31). Believer, let your manner of life be worthy of the gospel; stand firm in one spirit, with one mind, striving side by side for the faith of the gospel (Phil. 1:27), encouraged and strengthened by the life of Christ.

## Strengthened by Grace

The Galveston Hurricane of 1900 proved to be a day of reckoning for the small island. The state and the local residents couldn't continue to impotently strengthen the island by importing sand, raising homes on stilts, and planting trees to anchor the sand dunes in place. Galveston needed physical protection in weakness and courage to stand firm through future storms.

In 1902, the city finally began to construct a massive seawall. The 16-foot-wide wall stretched 10 miles long down the Galveston shore and stood 17 feet high; its strong facade protected the vulnerable city when storms came by holding the ocean at bay. In addition to building the seawall, 2,100 buildings were lifted up and the ground beneath was filled with sand that would physically raise the entire island. When the next category four hurricane hit Galveston 15 years later, the island stood firm. With the seawall, the city was stronger and better prepared to shelter its residents and its infrastructure from future destruction.

Since you are reading this book, let me affirm that I only finished writing it during a pandemic by the miraculous strength of God. God's grace carried me through homeschooling, moving, breaking bones, and catching illnesses, and helped me to be strong and courageous and just keep writing when I didn't know if I could continue. When I honestly wondered if I was strong enough to finish, God faithfully reminded me I wasn't. But he was.

When I wanted to give up, God's word encouraged me to confess my need to him and to seek help or accountability from a trusted friend. When I needed to cry, God gave me a friend who would listen. When I felt tempted to buckle down and strengthen myself, God did not let my plans pan out; he always knew the better way to deliver me from my own fear and selfish desires. God allowed me to face the discomfort of my need because he knew it would lead me to his better strength and encourage me to come quickly to him the next time a storm came.

When has life left you feeling vulnerable and exposed? How did God use the storm or the battle to strengthen you? Think of the ways you might have been tempted to fall away from obeying God or to fall headlong into temptation. Consider whether you tried to strengthen yourself or rested in the shelter of God's strength. When strong storms arise or you're invaded by an enemy you didn't see coming, how might you take practical steps to reinforce your heart in the strength of God?

Weakness teaches you to cling to God in moments of need. But encouragement strengthens you to continue holding on when you're worried you can't. God's encouragement strengthens and invigorates your heart in a way that stirs your desire so that you'll want to return again and again for more of God's help. God will encourage you to be strong and courageous and to stand firm when the waters come up to your neck. He will fill your life with countless daily mercies. Even if you don't feel stronger, God can strengthen you to keep showing up and laboring for his kingdom and glory. He is able to bless the labor of weary hands. If you look at your life and see a million ways where the enemy condemns and says you could have done better, choose to "be strong in the Lord and in the strength of his might." Friend, "it is good for the heart to be strengthened by grace" (Heb. 13:9) when it is the "grace that is in Christ Jesus" (2 Tim. 2:1).

6

# The Comfort of Encouragement

WHEN A FIFTY-YEAR-OLD man arrived in a Philadelphia emergency room reporting three days' worth of intermittent chest pain, his doctors were surprised to find in his initial physical exam that the man's chest was covered in a strange array of circular bruises.[1] While the cause of the bruising pattern was peculiar and not immediately identifiable, the doctors temporarily overlooked the external signs of trauma. Using electrocardiogram imaging, they examined the man's heart and immediately identified the source of his pain. He'd had a heart attack. One of his coronary arteries was completely blocked.

Blocked coronary arteries deprive the heart muscle of blood, oxygen, and nutrients that are essential in sustaining healthy human life. Without them, the heart muscle can be permanently damaged. The amount of damage done depends, in large part,

---

1   Gregory Marhefka and Michael Savage, "Medical Mystery: Chest Pain, A Heart Attack, and Odd Bruises," *The Philadelphia Inquirer*, October 16, 2016, https://www.inquirer.com/.

on how quickly the patient is able to receive intervention and treatment. Time is always of the essence.

But instead of seeking help at the onset of his pain by heading to the nearest emergency room, the man sought comfort on his own. Instead of healing, he sought temporary comfort in an Eastern medicine practice called "cupping."[2] By suctioning small heated glass globes above the source of his heart pain, he'd hoped to find physical relief. Instead, cupping had covered the man's chest in mysterious bruises that only added a confusing symptom to consider in his diagnosis. While cupping may encourage blood flow, increase circulation, promote healing, and reduce lower back pain, it wasn't the scientifically recommended course of treatment for unblocking a clogged coronary artery.

The man attempted to comfort himself, saying "peace, peace" when there was no peace (Jer. 6:14) because his heart muscle was in physical distress and he opted to be healed lightly. Cupping couldn't provide healing of this magnitude; it only delayed it. To save and sustain the patient's life, he needed a hospital, diagnostic expertise, a skilled surgeon, and a caring surgical support team.

In the Western world, when a patient seeks medical help, they usually assume that medical professionals will not only diagnose and treat their ailment but also keep the patient physically comfortable. We expect compassionate care to include pain management—the assurance that we are being cared for by qualified doctors and anesthesiologists who will manage our pain—before we agree to a scalpel entering our flesh.

2    Katie Rosenblum, "What is Cupping? Does it Work?" *Cedars-Sinai* (blog), January 13, 2020, https://www.cedars-sinai.org/.

When Christians are spiritually heartsick, we desire and instinctively yearn for the same assurance, compassion, and comfort for our soul. Proverbs 18:14 says, "A man's spirit will endure sickness, but a crushed spirit who can bear?" When Jeremiah fears his heart may fail, he seeks the Lord's help because he trusts that God will comfort him by relieving his distress: "Heal me, O LORD, and I shall be healed; save me, and I shall be saved . . . you are my refuge in the day of disaster" (Jer. 17:14, 17). If you are heartsick, you need more than what temporary comforts can provide—you need healing and comfort that lasts.

## Who Will Comfort Me?

The more people share in the same struggle, the more they share in similar comforts. This phenomenon was easily observable during the COVID-19 pandemic. Suddenly, when we were all trapped at home and coping with shared stressful circumstances, we could suffer with and relate to one another better than we had before. Social media posts provided us a rare glimpse into how other people were coping with discomfort.

When the days were long and the weeks were hard, I took comfort in leisurely walks in the fresh air, climbing and exploring the woods near our house with my kids. I listened to rich, edifying music and read thought-provoking books. I got in the habit of painting my nails. Much of my comfort came from maintaining daily routines and structure. My kids, on the other hand, preferred to take comfort in baking, watching movies, and playing outside. When we desired comfort more than ever, we somehow all managed to find our own coping mechanisms. We don't have to look very far to find someone or something that will comfort us in times of discouragement or pain.

Whether comfort exercise, comfort sleeping, comfort baking, comfort eating, comfort online shopping, or wearing comfy clothes and snuggling under comfy blankets is your preference, we all have our preferred pleasures and ways of watching out for our well-being. One survey reported that during pandemic living, "comfort food made a giant comeback" in America; the average person in quarantine enjoyed comfort meals at least five times a week.[3] And nearly 70 percent plan to continue these comfort measures even post-pandemic. Why?

"When things are uneasy, it's the little joys that get us through, whether that's FaceTiming with family and friends or stronger bonds made over home cooked meals," said Ciera Womack, who summarized the survey.[4] She continued, "as these responses show, sometimes it's seeking comfort in certain foods which provide us more relief."[5] More relief than what? As Christians, we know. We know that we are intended to seek comfort in the Lord and find encouragement in him. Now, before you panic and assume that I'm about to shame your comfort measures, don't worry, I'm not. I merely want you to consider how the pleasure you find in your existing comfort measures is meant to entice you to seek God's better comfort, which will heal you more than any other comfort you might be looking forward to.

---

3  "2020: The Year of the Comfort Food Comeback," *Cision*, September 22, 2020, https://www.prnewswire.com/.

4  "2020," *Cision*.

5  "2020," *Cision*.

We often struggle to answer the question, "Who will comfort me?" because we've been let down by the encouragement and comfort we've found from other people. Sometimes we wrongly assume that God's encouragement and comfort are equally disappointing. Other times, in an effort to love God and serve him only, we may be tempted to overcorrect in the other direction and refuse all measures of tangible comfort, as though an extreme form of monastic living that denies all pleasure is the way to holiness. But throughout Scripture, God provides physical measures of tangible comfort to his people through their relationships with one another: provision (grain, wine, milk, and honey), miraculous signs and wonders, and the observable comforts of nature. God provides abundant measures of comfort for his people. Who will comfort us? God will!

## Does No Balm Remain?

We tend to cringe about enjoying God's blessings and comfort provided for us in relationships, words, food, physical activity, entertainment, or physical touch because we've been bruised before. Whether we've been injured by the world's brokenness or our own sin, we fear we will be further injured or further injure ourselves in our search for comfort. We don't want to depend on comfort that could disappear at any time. And we don't want to misuse or idolize comforts either. But navigating all these challenges feels more complicated than simply ignoring our need for comfort. We must practice quickly inviting God's healing and comfort and receiving it with gratitude that does not flinch at the healer's kindness or begrudge his means of provision.

To comfort simply means to "to give strength and hope to" or "to ease the grief or trouble of."[6] Comfort cheers and consoles by offering assistance, support, or consolation in a time of worry. Sometimes, we would rather exclude God from the role of comforter because we're angry with him for allowing our weakness or grief. How can God comfort, cheer, or support us when our discomfort feels as though it came from his hand too?

In Genesis 27 Esau's mother and brother Jacob schemed against him in order to trick his father Isaac into blessing Jacob instead of Esau. When Esau realized what he'd lost, "he cried out with an exceedingly great and bitter cry and said to his father, 'Bless me, even me also, O my father,'" (27:34). Esau understood that Jacob would now become lord over him and inherit all his father's servants, grain, and wine. Why had God allowed this? Isaac's hands tied, he rhetorically asked Esau, "What then can I do for you, my son?" (27:37). In that moment, Esau wanted the comfort of his father's blessing more than he wanted anything else.

Betrayed and heartsick, Esau lifted up his voice and wept. But when his desire for justice, additional blessings, and immediate relief was not filled, he took matters into his own hands and sought comfort on his own. In Genesis 27:42 Esau's mother Rebekah warned her younger son Jacob, "Behold, your brother Esau comforts himself about you by planning to kill you." The Hebrew meaning behind the phrase "comforts himself" implies that Esau's actions were an attempt "to pity, console . . . reflexively rue," or "avenge" himself.[7] He comforted himself by making

---

6    *Merriam-Webster*, s.v. "comfort, (*v.*)," accessed September 29, 2021, https://www.merriam
     -webster.com/.

7    *Blue Letter Bible*, "נָחַם," accessed September 29, 2021, https://www.blueletterbible.org/.

Jacob and his mother "rue the day" of his betrayal. When Esau took comfort in the form of his own bad medicine, his spirit was crushed (Prov. 15:13).

Think of the last time you experienced a season of painful discouragement. Have you ever set out to read Scripture, attend your local church's Sunday gathering, or recommit to an accountability relationship with another Christian friend in order to find the encouragement and comfort you knew you needed but were tempted to give up when your investment didn't immediately yield comfort or courage? When God's promises or counsel fail to feel comforting to your spirit, are you tempted to turn instead to lesser measures like shopping, entertainment, or food? You may not think of abandoning spiritual disciplines as a punitive response to discomfort, but when we avoid looking to God for his comfort, it's often our own rebellious way of angrily conveying our disappointment to God. We can't humbly request his comfort while passive-aggressively shaking our fist at him in frustration.

Bitterness is bad medicine that won't yield any relief. When we mourn like the prophet in Jeremiah 8:22, complaining that our joy is gone, grief is upon us, and our heart is sick, we need God to convince us that there is a balm in Gilead and we have a physician who desires to heal and comfort us.

### Better Comfort Heals

As God's people we can think of Christian discouragement as a treatable heartsickness that our Father is always on top of. When our spirit is wounded and we seek God's comfort, he provides us with a better standard of care. He manages our overall spiritual health, healing and comforting even when we don't know how to diagnose, treat, or help our own hearts. God sees deeper than our bruises and surface-level injuries and knows exactly how to encourage and comfort us before we even ask.

The God of encouragement "is a physician good at all diseases, especially at the binding up of a broken heart."[8] His better encouragement enables you to believe the words of Psalm 94:18–19 that say when your foot slips and the cares of your heart are many, God's love and consolations are able to cheer your soul. You can't pursue the Lord's healing while rejecting the tenderness of his comfort. The Lord enables healing and comfort to work in tandem because he knows that you require both to be made whole.

Throughout this book I've pointed out that the battle cry "be strong and courageous" is an encouragement that calls God's people into faithful obedience and action. But inside the battle cry of Deuteronomy 31 lies a relational message intended for our comfort. Verse 8 says, "It is the LORD who goes before you. He will be with you; he will not leave you or forsake you. Do not fear or be dismayed." These words effectively encourage God's people because they connect the soldiers to the love and compassion of the King who calls them into battle. The exhortation sends Christians into the battle against sin, suffering, and darkness, fully equipped and armed with the promises of God while also gently assuring fearful soldiers of the Lord's comforting presence.

When King David exhorts his son Solomon in 1 Chronicles 22:13 to build God's house and obediently fulfill the statutes of God, he encourages him with these words: "Be strong and courageous. Fear not; do not be dismayed." Our eyes are naturally

---

8    Richard Sibbes, *The Bruised Reed* (Edinburg: Banner of Truth Trust, 2018), 8.

drawn to the instruction "fear not" because we want to please God, but we aren't so sure what to make of the dismay part. What does dismay mean? In Deuteronomy 31:8, the Hebrew word for dismayed is *hatat*. Sound familiar? It's the same word used throughout Scripture to describe discouragement. It means to be prostrated and broken down or to abolish.

The Hebrew word for "courageous" is *amets*, which means "to be alert, physically (on foot) or mentally (in courage)" or "to be of good courage, steadfastly minded."[9] Weakness, anxieties, insecurities, fears, and suffering threaten to rob our hearts of the ability to stand firm and remain alert or engaged. We become heartsick because we are prostrated by our doubt and unbelief. In seasons of spiritual illness, we require the better medicine of God's comforting promises to nurse us back to faith and obedience by providing us with "good courage."

God's people are filled with good courage through the encouragement of God's comfort. Without these mercies, we aren't equipped to be strong or courageous. Instead, we will be prostrated, broken down, and disheartened (2 Cor. 4:1) because, on our own, our hearts are broken cisterns (Jer. 2:13) whose cracks and wounds cannot be healed lightly by saying "Peace, peace" (Jer. 6:14). Because we are easily discouraged, God trains us to come quickly to him for comfort at the first signs of pain or emptiness! For Christians, discouragement is like spiritual heart disease— we need the healer's wise intervention and gentle comfort. God will diagnose and treat the deeper wounds of our soul that we cannot see on our own; he will unblock the unbelief or sin that

---

9   *Blue Letter Bible*, "אָמֵץ," accessed September 29, 2021, https://www.blueletterbible.org/.

plagues our hearts and minds, and he will heal and comfort the weak and tender places where we've been drained of the good nourishment of his promises.

God saves his people through the victory of Christ in order to encourage them to trust Christ when he calls them into battle. As you go into all the world, he knows that you're already bruised and bleeding from the world's brokenness and your own indwelling sin. Christ expects your weakness to appear throughout the course of battle. When you trip or are taken down by battle wounds, you are not alone or unprotected. Because Christ goes with you, you have ongoing care and comfort from the Spirit who is your ever-present Helper. God will heal you (Ex. 15:26) and comfort you (2 Cor. 7:7) as you fight to stand firm. God's healing is good medicine that cheers our soul.

## Better Comfort in Christ

Christ's example of suffering encourages us to persevere when the course of treatment seems too extensive and the comfort too far off. God's timeline is not ours. While we may pray for the comfort of immediate relief and healing, expediency isn't always the blessing God has ordained. In these moments of waiting, better encouragement comforts us by way of the cross. Because we share in the suffering of Christ, we have the ongoing comfort of Christ's encouragement in our fellowship with him. Because Christ was no stranger to heartache and rejection, his life models the comfort of his better encouragement.

In Isaiah 61, the prophet Isaiah proclaimed the good news of the coming Messiah to Israel to assure them of the better comforter who was to come. More than four hundred years later, Jesus fulfilled the prophecy when he began his public ministry. After he returned from being tested in the wilderness, he stood before the synagogue on the Sabbath "in the power of the Spirit" and proclaimed, "The Spirit of the Lord is upon me, because he has anointed me to proclaim good news to the poor. He has sent me to proclaim liberty to the captives and recovering of sight to the blind, to set at liberty those who are oppressed, to proclaim the year of the Lord's favor" (Luke 4:14, 18–19). If the people had listened with ears of faith, they would have heard the encouraging words that God had finally sent his comforter. But they were too busy looking for someone better.

When Joseph's son claimed to be the Messiah, every eye in his hometown landed on him in scrutiny, confident that his proclamation couldn't be the actual fulfillment of Scripture. After the men marveled at the words, Jesus explained more. They became angrier and angrier and eventually threw stones at him to drive him out of town. Even though the Father had given Jesus the authority to comfort his people, the men lacked the faith to believe Jesus was the Christ and so they failed to take comfort in the one God had appointed to speak tenderly to Jerusalem (Isa. 40:1–2).

Jesus wasn't discouraged by the unfavorable outcome of his ministry's beginning. He wasn't distracted from fulfilling the Father's plans. He simply got up, left the town, and continued the work set before him. He was frequently moved to labor in the kingdom because he saw the crowd of people with all of their needs and felt compassion for them. In Matthew 5:4, during the Sermon on the Mount, Jesus taught the crowd to view blessing in a different manner than they had before. Rather than striving for strength and boldness of spirit, Jesus said, "Blessed are those who mourn, for they shall be comforted."

Here, the word "comforted" is the Greek word *parakaleō,* which means "to call near, invite, invoke by consolation," or call to be of good comfort.[10] Christ came to earth to call sinners to repentance with his gentle words of consolation. God's people could be healed and comforted fully, in lasting measure, through the promise of redemption. Christ would be victorious in the battle against sin and death, even when the strength of the individual soldiers failed. The sting of sin and the curse of death no longer have a vicious hold on the heartsick. Now, Christ calls his people near for aid, exhorting them to "take heart."

Jesus first spoke these words to a paralytic man when a group of people carried him to Jesus for healing in Matthew 9:2. Scripture says that Jesus "saw their faith" and said to the paralytic, "Take heart, my son; your sins are forgiven." Again, in Matthew 9:22 when the woman with the discharge of blood reached out and touched the fringe of Jesus's garment, he responded with the same words of exhortation that he'd spoken to the paralyzed man: "Take heart." And when blind Bartimaeus cried out, "Jesus, Son of David, have mercy on me!" even the disciples responded, "Take heart. Get up; he is calling you" (Luke 18:38; Mark 10:49).

Christ's encouragement to "take heart" uses the Greek word *tharseō,* which means "to be of good courage, cheer, or comfort."[11] In Matthew 14:27, when Christ's disciples saw him walking on

---

10 *Blue Letter Bible*, "παρακαλέω," accessed September 29, 2021, https://www.blueletterbible.org/.

11 *Blue Letter Bible*, "θαρσέω," accessed September 29, 2021, https://www.blueletterbible.org/.

water and were terrified, Jesus comforted them by saying, "Take heart; it is I. Do not be afraid." And when Jesus comforted his disciples and prepared them for his death in John 16:33, he said, "In the world you will have tribulation. But take heart; I have overcome the world." Jesus didn't demand spiritual strength; he comforted his people in their weakness by reminding them of *his* strength. When Christ calls us to take heart in the promise that "neither death nor life, nor angels nor rulers, nor things present nor things to come, nor powers, nor height nor depth, nor anything else in all creation, will be able to separate us from the love of God in Christ Jesus our Lord" (Rom. 8:38–39), we should be encouraged by his words of comfort because they show us that we will not remain sick, wounded, or broken forever. We will be made whole.

## The Encouragement That Comfort Delivers

After my friend Katharine suffered a miscarriage, her heart was understandably broken and bruised. She'd been open about her loss within her local community of believers and she and her husband had friends all over the country who were praying for them as they grieved. One particularly difficult morning, Katharine walked four blocks from her house to catch the bus to work. As she waited, she happened to glance at the ground and notice a rain-soaked, handwritten letter that had been torn out of its envelope and carelessly discarded on the sidewalk. It was addressed to "Katharine."

Immediately noting how odd it was to find a letter at her bus stop written to someone who happened to spell their name exactly as she did, she began to read it out of curiosity. The letter had been lovingly written for the purpose of encouraging a friend in her faith as she walked through the pain of her recent miscarriage. The soggy letter she held in her hands had been intended for her, sent by one of her friends from another state.

Later, Katharine would learn the note had been inside a care package of thoughtful gifts that someone had apparently stolen from her doorstep, opened, and then discarded on the rain-soaked streets of Seattle. When Katharine arrived home from work that night, there was the mangled box, waiting for her on her doorstep. A neighbor must have found and returned it. When Katharine's heart was broken and yearning for the encouragement of the Lord, the Spirit comforted her in the morning through a soggy letter from a friend and in the evening through the return of the battered box. God capably preseved Katharine through the rain, and not even the powers of darkness could steal the comfort of her encouragement. Friend, God promises to encourage and comfort you too.

As followers of Jesus, we are able to rejoice in suffering because "the Lord has comforted his people and will have compassion on his afflicted" (Isa. 49:13). Fresh on the heels of Paul's persecution in Asia, he refers to God in 2 Corinthians 1:3–4 as "the Father of mercies and God of all comfort, who comforts us in all our affliction." When Paul was "so utterly burdened beyond [his] strength that [he] despaired of life itself," he rejoiced because of how abundantly he had shared in Christ's comfort (2 Cor. 1:8). Christ encourages us by providing his comfort and convincing us to repeatedly take heart in him.

I shared in the previous chapter that as I finished writing the final draft of this book manuscript, I did so with my arm in a sling and the fevered body aches I acquired from COVID-19. As

I petitioned the Lord for strength and help, I looked earnestly for the encouragement of his comfort because I trusted that he would comfort me again (Ps. 71:21). One particularly difficult day, an email arrived in my inbox. Inside, there was an UberEats digital gift card from my friend Katharine to purchase dinner for our family of seven so that we wouldn't have to worry about making or picking up dinner when we were sick. When I felt ill and miserable, an Uber driver delivered food to our doorstep; but God had clearly been the one to deliver the encouragement of his comfort to my heart. That night, I "derived much joy and comfort" from the love of my friend Katharine because her encouragement refreshed my heart in Christ (Philem. 1:7).

Because Christ's ability to sympathize is not "cool, detached pity" but "a depth of felt solidarity,"[12] better encouragement must comfort believers by reinforcing the depths of Christ's attention and love for his people. In Dane Ortlund's book *Gentle and Lowly*, he explains that "Jesus sits close" when we need relief the most and he will not "lob down a pep-talk from Heaven . . . [or] hold himself at a distance."[13]

Christian, you have endless access to an immediate source of comfort because you have an "all sufficient comforter in Christ."[14] The God of encouragement encourages you with his comfort so that you will encourage and comfort one another "with the comfort with which we ourselves are comforted by God" (2 Cor. 1:4). Take heart; Christ has overcome the world.

---

12 Dane Ortlund, *Gentle and Lowly: The Heart of Christ for Sinners and Sufferers* (Wheaton, IL: Crossway, 2020), 46.

13 Ortlund, *Gentle and Lowly*, 48, 50.

14 Sibbes, *Bruised Reed*, 66.

# 7

# The Hope of Encouragement

ELBERT AND MAURINE STARTUP of Irvine, California encouraged their eleven children to believe that if they dreamed big enough and worked hard enough they could accomplish anything they set their hopes on. Decades later, the couple's youngest daughter DeAnne recounted a poignant moment in her childhood when her mother returned home from work with an object lesson that would stick with her forever. Her mother gathered all eleven children at the bottom of the stairs and instructed them to close their eyes. On her command, she called the children to look up. When they did, their mother stood above them, tossing fistfuls of cash into the air.[1]

Maurine pulled three thousand dollars' worth of small bills from her purse and tossed them over the heads of her mesmerized children, and as the money rained down her daughter DeAnne recalled hearing her mother's instructions: "Pick it all up! Whatever

---

[1] *LuLaRich*, episode 1, "Start Up," directed and produced by Julia Willoughby Nason and Jenner Furst, aired September 10, 2021 on Amazon Prime Video.

you want! It's yours! Mom did this for you! We're going to go shopping! We're going to get ice cream!"[2] Maurine's grand gesture of generosity taught DeAnne that hard work paid off and encouraged her to hope for whatever her heart desired: business success, money, fame, fortune, or happiness.

As an adult, DeAnne found she had to work harder than she'd expected to lay hold of what she'd always wanted. Life wasn't easy as a young single mother of seven when dollar bills weren't falling from the sky. At times, she longed to buy her children the cute clothes she couldn't afford while she scraped pennies together to get them hamburgers off the dollar menu. But around 2013, DeAnne's life turned a corner as her hope appeared on the horizon. After selling skirts out of the back of her car trunk, her budding business endeavor unexpectedly burst into a billion-dollar dream come true. Four years later, DeAnne's multilevel-marketing clothing company had onboarded 100,000 sales representatives and garnered 2.83 billion dollars in revenue.[3] Finally, hope seemed to have dawned for DeAnne as money began to fall from the sky. At least, that's the part of the story she likes to tell in order to inspire others.

People like success stories because they lead us to hope. When a person gives us the chance to dream about laying hold of what we do not currently possess, we feel hopeful, filled with the anticipation of coming good. If a friend, family member, business owner, mentor, or teacher encourages us to believe that we have good reason to hope, we are usually willing to try anything. We will attempt to change our eating habits, get up earlier, tighten

2   *LuLaRich*, episode 1.
3   *LuLaRich*, episode 1.

our wallets, and work longer hours if doing so extends our ability to reach a promised reward.

But if the Christian's primary source of encouragement is not the God of encouragement and endurance—as defined, declared, and displayed through the authority of Holy Scripture—then can Christ be her true source of hope? God's people are meant to wait with hope by the encouragement of the one in whom our soul trusts. Oh saint, why are you hopeless? Where do you take courage? In whom do you place your trust?

## The Good Intentions of Hope

Hebrews 11:1 says that "faith is the assurance of things hoped for, the conviction of things not seen." But Christians do not always think about how often they pluck this scripture and apply it as truth over their own worldly desires and assumptions. For instance, if money and career success are what we hope for, then we frequently pursue encouragement that assures us that if we have faith in our business model, product, team, and timeline, we have every reason to expect success—we can hope to gather a good reward.

As a college student I spent my summer break working for a radio station. One afternoon between shows, a coworker sat down to eat lunch and visit. I expected a casual, polite conversation about our weekends. Instead, he unloaded the weariness of his soul over sandwiches. He and his wife were teenagers when they married and neither were believers. When he recently came to faith, she became angry and hostile. She wanted no part of Jesus or the church. My friend begged God to save his wife and his marriage and to use their story for his glory. But over the weekend, she

had handed him divorce papers, loaded all her belongings into his pickup truck, grabbed their dog, and drove away into the sunset.

My friend's flat, expressionless words dripped with hopeless resignation. He worried he would never marry again. Never have children. Never be happy. Never be used by God. Never heal from the loss and brokenness. And never laugh again or feel the joy or peace of God. He hadn't just lost his wife, his dog, and his hope of having a family together—he'd lost the hope that God could heal, redeem, and fill his life with good blessings. My friend's discouragement had robbed him of the ability to hope in God. He hadn't turned away from God; he was simply too afraid and dismayed to trust God's promises when they said that he could look with hope to the future.

I wanted to encourage my friend, but I didn't know how. At that time, I was a nineteen-year-old college student and a relatively new believer. I had zero marital wisdom or relational advice to offer but I opened my mouth and attempted to encourage him anyway. I spoke the words I knew he wanted to hear. I told my friend I was sure that God had the perfect wife for him. Surely, either God would save his current wife and lead her back to the marriage or would one day provide him with a new wife who loved Jesus. My friend's eyes filled with tears of gratitude and he thanked me for my words of encouragement. In between writing radio commercial spots, I creatively wrote my friend a reason to hope that was based solely on the reward of my own good intentions.

## Christians Hope in God

In the 1998 Forest Whitaker movie *Hope Floats*, Sandra Bullock's character Birdee Pruitt counsels her young daughter Bernice

who's struggling to find peace and joy in a new school and a new town that she's been forced to move to after her parents' recent divorce. Looking into Bernice's sad, tear-filled eyes, Pruitt says: "Beginnings are scary, endings are usually sad, but it is the middle that counts the most. You need to remember that when you find yourself at the beginning. Just give hope a chance to float up."[4]

As cute and well-received as the movie was back then, Pruitt's advice still stands out in my mind as being just about as cringe-worthy as the advice I gave to my friend after his wife left. This encouragement provides no promise, no provider of good, and no blessing or reward except that of waiting around for some generic sense of better. Hope cannot possibly encourage God's people when we believe that it is a resource we're simply waiting around for without any pursuit or investment. Biblical hope is not meant to just float up out of nowhere whenever it pleases because it is not a vague or intangible resource.

When Christians do not understand hope, we are likely to view it as though it is an ambiguous tool that may or may not be specifically helpful to us because we aren't confident about where to look to find it or what kind of hope honors God. When we don't know how to "hold fast" to hope, we will forget how to endure until he comes (Rev. 2:25). We must be reminded by God how to endure with hope. God helps us hold onto hope by clearly defining it so it isn't ambiguous or unattainable. The psalmist pleads in Psalm 119:49–50, "Remember your word to your servant, in which you have made me hope. This is my

---

4   *Hope Floats*, directed by Forest Whitaker, May 29, 1998, 20th Century Fox.

comfort in my affliction, that your promise gives me life." God's promises lead us to hope in him.

When Hezekiah became sick and Isaiah the prophet visited to inform him that the Lord wanted him to set his house in order in preparation for his death, Hezekiah prayed and wept bitterly, "Please, O LORD, remember how I have walked before you in faithfulness and with a whole heart, and have done what is good in your sight" (Isa. 38:3). The Lord heard Hezekiah's prayer, saw his tears, added fifteen years to his life, and promised to deliver him and his city from the king of Assyria (Isa. 38:2–6). After the Lord delivered Hezekiah and he had returned to health, Hezekiah wrote:

> Behold, it was for my welfare that I had great bitterness; but in love you have delivered my life from the pit of destruction, for you have cast all my sins behind your back. For Sheol does not thank you; death does not praise you; those who go down to the pit do not hope for your faithfulness. The living, the living, he thanks you, as I do this day; the father makes known to the children your faithfulness. (Isa. 38:17–19)

God provides his words and his promises to encourage his people to hope exclusively in him. When we know that we are uniquely encouraged to hope in God, we will be prompted to boast in his faithfulness. We gain confidence to trust that he will fulfill his promises and provide us with rewards only known to those who are his. Christian hope is not vague, indistinguishable, or undesirable; rather, God assures us that our hope in him is certain, distinguishable, and endlessly desirable.

## Jesus, Our Better Hope

In the Old Testament, biblical hope filled God's people with his promises to help them endure for the future with their hope set on him (Prov. 24:14). Before Christ came to earth, Israel hoped for a savior and waited by God's promises. But when the Word became flesh and dwelt among us in the person of Jesus, we saw the glory of the Father, full of grace and truth, and received "grace upon grace" from the fullness of God (John 1:16). God has strengthened the Christian's ability to hope in his promises by sending his Son.

Romans 5:1–2 explains that since we have been "justified by faith, we have peace with God through our Lord Jesus Christ" and have also "obtained access by faith into this grace in which we stand, and we rejoice *in hope of the glory of God.*" Because Christ adopted us into the family of God and secured our ability to hope in God forever, he encourages us to aim our hope in the direction of God's glory. Because "Christ is faithful over God's house as a son," we demonstrate that we are a part of his household of faith by holding fast to our confidence in Christ and by boasting of our hope in him (Heb. 3:6). We are supposed to hope and earnestly long to see the glory of our Father more than we long for earthly riches, success, fame, or anything else.

As we struggle with sin, suffering, and discouragement, and we long and yearn for the resurrection of our earthly body, do we wait as people who recognize our reason for hope? Do we look eagerly to the promise of our coming new life in Christ? Or are we more encouraged to hope in the world's temporary promises because we underestimate the hope we're meant to find through

Christ's resurrection? When we lose sight of hope, Christ's life is meant to serve as our better encouragement. While our obedience to the law couldn't offer us any hope, Hebrews 7:19 assures us that through Christ, "a better hope is introduced." Jesus is our better hope because he has given us a way to draw near to God and is the guarantor of the better covenant.

We need regular reminders of our reason for encouragement and hope. "The God of endurance and encouragement" provides us with his word, which was "written in former days . . . for our instruction" in order to help us understand how tempted we are to lose sight of the gospel and to forget our reason for hope (Rom. 15:4–5). We must cling to hope by clinging to Christ as our ongoing source of encouragement. Titus 3:4–7 explains that when

> the goodness and loving kindness of God our Savior appeared, he saved us, not because of works done by us in righteousness, but according to his own mercy, by the washing of regeneration and renewal of the Holy Spirit, whom he poured out on us richly through Jesus Christ our Savior, so that being justified by his grace we might become heirs according to the hope of eternal life.

Christ reminds his people that without faith it is impossible to please him. But when we come to him, believing in him for salvation, he will reward us when we diligently seek him (Heb. 11:6). Christ is our better hope of salvation, our better hope of redemption, and our hope of new life.

We are better encouraged to wait with our hope fixed on Jesus, "through the Spirit, by faith," as we "eagerly wait for the hope of righteousness" (Gal. 5:5). We are able to hope in the power of

Christ at work on our behalf that through the Spirit our bodies will be made whole in the resurrection. This truth encourages us to wait with hope even through our sufferings. Our pain will not last forever and it cannot compare to the glory set before us in heaven. Christ encourages us to hope, even in our waiting and our suffering. When we look to the life and death of Christ, we are able to better understand how we might apply the encouragement of Christ, who is the hope by which we are saved (Rom. 8:24).

### The Power of Hope's Encouragement

In Matthew 8:23, Jesus and his disciples were in a boat when a great storm rose on the sea. The waves threatened to swamp the boat and the men feared they would be thrown overboard and left to die. Jesus, weary from the previous journey, was sleeping through the storm. Rather than feeling comforted by his peace in the raging storm, the men were terrified. As the waves crashed inside their boat, the fishermen were likely imagining worst-case scenarios. If Jesus didn't wake up soon, surely the storm would overtake the boat, the waves would overtake the men, and they would all die. No hope remained. Well, no hope of their own remained.

When all the men's hope was exhausted, they finally woke up Jesus. These men were professional fishermen with years' worth of collective wisdom and experience in massive storms. They probably felt the responsibility to manage the situation on their own. But they would have also understood the danger of that specific storm and, from an earthly perspective, had real reason to fear the storm. However, their hope wasn't intended to be based on the height of the waves or the power of the winds. It should have been fixed on the Savior who was sleeping in their boat. The disciples lacked the ability to hope in God's power to sustain their lives in the midst of the storm. They assumed that because Jesus was asleep, God was off duty.

The disciples' instinctive hope in Christ wasn't what bubbled to the surface when the men were under pressure. Instead, they displayed fear and panic when they were the ones who required personal rescue. When they cried out, "Save us, Lord; we are perishing," their hopeless resignation showed (8:25). They assumed they were dying, not that Christ would powerfully save them even without their panicked cries. Jesus, waking from his slumber, did not act confused, annoyed, or startled. He asked the men a question: "Why are you afraid, O you of little faith?" (8:26). I'm sure the disciples didn't appreciate the timing of this life lesson. But as the seas raged, Jesus addressed their lack of faith first. And then he rose and rebuked the winds and the sea and there was a great calm.

When Jesus was under pressure, he displayed perfect love and perfect peace. He heard the men's cries and responded gently. Teaching moment first, then rescue and relief later. Jesus provided the men with the salvation they hoped for, and by giving them the calmed waters and winds, he provided them with even more peace than they had asked for. In response, the men marveled and asked, "What sort of man is this, that even winds and sea obey him?" (8:27).

It wasn't as though the disciples had needed to see a miracle to hope in Jesus. They spent more time with Jesus than anyone. They had a better chance to listen to his stories and glean from his wisdom. They had better seats at the dinner table and better access to all of the miracles. Even though they saw Christ heal diseases, cast out demons, and give sight to the blind, their faith in Jesus still wavered and was weak under pressure.

Christ's power over the winds and waves taught the disciples to hope in his power over their lives and their fears. In the storm, Christ had given them the ability to rest in his peace and to "ascribe power to God" (Ps. 68:34) even when they were afraid. Their panic was evidence of their hopelessness and doubt, even though God had always held the power over the winds and sea. Psalm 107:25–32 reminds us that God

> commanded and raised the stormy wind, which lifted up the waves of the sea. [The redeemed] mounted up to heaven; they went down to the depths; their courage melted away in their evil plight; they reeled and staggered like drunken men and were at their wits' end. Then they cried to the LORD in their trouble, and he delivered them from their distress. He made the storm be still, and the waves of the seas were hushed. Then they were glad that the waters were quiet, and he brought them to their desired haven. Let them thank the LORD for his steadfast love, for his wondrous works to the children of man! Let them extol him in the congregation of the people, and praise him in the assembly of the elders.

The disciples' little faith should encourage our hearts by bringing to light two existing realities about ourselves. We will all wrestle with little faith. But when we do, the Lord remains the source of our hope, our salvation, and our peace. Let us thank him for his steadfast love and praise him.

It's not our success stories that should encourage others to turn to the Lord for hope, salvation, and peace. Our stories of God's faithfulness and power in our moments of little faith provide a far better, more convincing hope. These are the stories that weak and broken sinners can relate to and find joy in. We must encourage one another by the hope of the Spirit, who is able to powerfully work in the hearts of the bruised and broken. Better encouragement reminds sinners to hope in Jesus's powerful peace when the winds and waves seem overwhelming.

## Encouraged to Wait for the Reward

The gospel of Jesus Christ radically redefines what we consider a worthy reward and when we hope to be rewarded. When Christians are filled with the Spirit of the risen Lord, we know "the hope to which he has called" us and we eagerly anticipate "the riches of his glorious inheritance" (Eph. 1:18).

Abraham obtained the promise of his inheritance after having "patiently waited" (Heb. 6:15). The Lord knows how to give good gifts to his people in his perfect timing. He provides earthly blessings here and now in this life. And he provides other blessings of our inheritance and promised rewards to those "who have fled for refuge" when we are united with him in resurrection (Heb. 6:18). God determines how and when he will provide us with his good gifts. We can always trust that he provides his "strong encouragement to hold fast to the hope set before us" (Heb. 6:18). We do not define the hope set before us. God has already done this for us. Because Jesus is our hope and peace, Jesus must remain the hope of our encouragement.

After Peter writes "Blessed be the God and Father of our Lord Jesus Christ!" and says that it's according to his great mercy that we've been born again, the apostle encourages Christians by exhorting them to trust Christ as their "living hope" (1 Pet. 1:3). The reason that Christian hope is better than any hope that we might find in the world is because it is active, moving, working within us, changing us, maturing us, and growing us in Christ. Living hope is incapable of being squelched, snuffed out, extinguished, or stopped. And, living hope provides an inheritance "that is imperishable, undefiled, and unfading, kept in heaven for you" (1:4).

Knowing that we have Christ's living hope and an imperishable inheritance that Christ is guarding for us in heaven reminds us that the tangible riches of this world are not our only hope of reward. We have not been alienated from God and our inheritance has not been withheld when we do not have the life we thought we would; this world is not our home. When we worry that God has withheld his blessing, we are reminded that "hope does not put us to shame, because God's love has been poured into our hearts through the Holy Spirit" (Rom. 5:5). The bridegroom will not put his bride to shame as she waits to be gathered to his side. We can hearken to Jesus with hope, trusting that he "who promises to make the wilderness like Eden, and the desert like the garden of the Lord" will reward us.[5]

## Encouraged by Hope

Money encouraged Maurine and her daughter DeAnne to hope in hard work and business success. When DeAnne's company recruited independent sales representatives to host private parties in their homes and sell their "buttery soft"[6] magic leggings across

---

5  Charles Haddon Spurgeon, "The Present Truth," in *The Metropolitan Tabernacle Pulpit: Sermons Preached and Revised During the Year 1881* (London: Pilgrim Publications), 242.

6  Elizabeth Armstrong Moore, "LuLaRoe Faces Lawsuit Over 'Buttery Soft' Leggings," *Fox News*, April 4, 2017, https://www.foxnews.com/.

the country, they encouraged women to buy into the company by successfully selling them the chance to hope. Women eagerly bought into her business, despite exorbitant startup costs, because DeAnne's company offered the hope of a better life. The company's marketing videos seemed to promise a sisterhood rather than a work environment, a full-time income on part-time hours, and a side hustle that wouldn't steal moms away from their families.

The company's promises successfully tugged at the heartstrings of hopeful women's deepest desires. If DeAnne could build an empire and go from dollar-menu hamburgers to diamonds, then perhaps they could build a better life too. Sadly, DeAnne's leggings empire didn't last because her promises turned out to be too good to be true. Many of the women who joined with the hope of finding a community of friends, a part-time income, and a better life for their family were left with only unsold leggings and remorse.

Christian, you will work for what you hope for. The Lord is your portion. Hope in him. In whatever you do, "work heartily, as for the Lord and not for men, knowing that from the Lord you will receive the inheritance as your reward" (Col. 3:23–24).

When Christ becomes the substance of your hope (1 Tim. 1:1), he will become your "hope of glory" (Col. 1:27). I once asked my older and wiser friend Nancy how God encouraged her to hope in him. She told me the story of how the Lord opened her eyes and called her to faith at the age of fifty-two, after twenty years of marriage, but she still had so "little faith" in God's ability to soften the heart of her unbelieving husband Bill. She remembers adamantly telling God, "There is no way you will save my husband. His heart is too hard."

For a while, Bill showed no interest in Nancy's newfound faith. He didn't want to talk to her about Jesus or understand what she'd been learning; instead he made regular comments about how strange it was that his wife of twenty years had somehow become a religious fanatic overnight. But Nancy's faith continued to grow, undeterred by Bill's annoyance. She continued to seek the wisdom and mercy of God. Each morning, she woke up in the early hours before Bill was awake in order to hide in the kitchen to study her Bible in secret, away from her husband's disapproving scrutiny. She joined a local church, started attending weekly, signed up for a women's Bible study, and even began serving inside the body of believers.

One morning as Nancy prepared to leave for church, her husband appeared beside her in the kitchen and asked, "What do I need to do to go to church with you?" Nancy admitted that even though God had softened her heart of stone, she was still shocked when her husband expressed interest in church out of the blue, totally unprovoked by any prodding of her own. All Nancy did was advise him to put on a suit and tie and get in the car. Over the next year and a half, Bill began to attend church regularly. He learned from the exposition of Scripture. He was discipled by godly men from their local church family. Eventually, God led Bill to repentance, faith, and salvation, just a few years before his death.

By saving Nancy's husband, God convinced her to hope in him for the seemingly impossible. Today, Nancy is one of the most encouraging women I know. And while she may have learned to initially hope in God because he saved her husband, her ongoing hope in Christ's mercy is the fruit of years and years of faithful pursuit of his wisdom and glory. Over time, Nancy has learned to hope in the encouragement of God by regularly studying the character and promises of God and taking heart directly from his word. As she is richly encouraged by the hope of God's promises, she is compelled to encourage others by the same words and promises of hope.

Nancy's hope in Jesus regularly leads her into difficult conversations and prompts her to share Christ with anyone who will listen. She presents the hope of resurrection to her unbelieving family members, next-door neighbors, and friends as though evangelism is as natural to her as breathing. When Nancy encourages the people she loves by the hope of Christ, she doesn't sound like she's trying to sell something. Her words are genuine and filled with love because she believes that Christ is truly her greatest reward.

Better encouragement calls the discouraged to rise up, take heart, and trust the God of hope who rewards the faith of those who love him. We don't need fame, success, dollar bills falling from the sky, or any empty promises that life on earth is sure to get better. When we hope in Christ, our reward is "greater wealth than the treasures of Egypt" (Heb. 11:26).

8

# The Unity of Encouragement

OLYMPIC ATHLETE ISAIAH JEWETT arrived at the Tokyo Olympic Games ready to win.[1] As one of the world's most skilled athletes, he'd spent his life working and training for this moment and the extraordinary opportunity. This was his chance to shine and stand out among all the other skilled runners, win the illustrious gold medal, and showcase his talent to the watching world.

But this wasn't how Jewett's story unfolded. Rather than effortlessly advancing past his eight-hundred-meter semifinals and onto a chance at gold, Jewett's hopes and dreams came to a crashing halt as a passing competitor accidentally tripped over him, causing both to fall to the ground. But viewers were pleasantly surprised by what happened next. Jewett extended his hand to his opponent. The two runners pulled each other back onto their feet, linked arms, and jogged together to the finish line. The runner who tripped Jewett allowed him to finish one step ahead.

---

1   Gary Klein, "U.S. Runner Isaiah Jewett Falls in 800-Meter Semifinals, Then Embodies the Olympic Spirit," *Los Angeles Times*, August 1, 2021, https://www.latimes.com/.

This kind of good sportsmanship is not unheard of among the community of professional runners. When New Zealand runner Nikki Hamblin crashed into United States rival Abbey D'Agostino in the 2016 Rio Olympics and both fell to the ground, audiences were moved when D'Agostino offered Hamblin her hand despite her own injury and helped her off the turf before shuffling to the finish line where the two would embrace. Hamblin later expressed pride that she could be "both a competitor and kind and responsive at the same time."[2]

Stories like these remind us of our own fragile humanity, that we are always less in control of outcomes than we'd like to be. Whether we are weak or strong, we are all capable of tripping and falling along the course, no matter how skilled we are or how hard we've trained. When we do, we will have the opportunity to get up and keep running for ourselves and our own glory or to get up and lend a helping hand to others who have fallen.

As a runner in the race of faith, what is the goal of your race? Do you desire encouragement in order to get ahead? Or do you desire encouragement in order to work together with your fellow runners? As a follower of Jesus, you are a member of the body of Christ; every other Christian in the body is a fellow team member whose name is recorded on the roster and who runs alongside you in the same race of faith. You have pledged to run together with the people of God under the headship of Christ.

---

2    Rick Maese, "They Were Strangers at the Starting Line. Less Than 20 Minutes Later, They Were Eternally Linked," *Washington Post*, August 16, 2016, https://www.washingtonpost.com/.

## Encouraged to Run Together

Paul implores Christians in 2 Corinthians 6:1 to run together so as not to "receive the grace of God in vain," putting no obstacle in anyone's way so that no fault may be found with our ministry but as servants of God, commending others to Christ. Because God listens to his people's cries and responds with salvation, we can faithfully respond by looking out for the needs of other runners as we run, willingly removing obstacles from the road or lending a hand to those who are weary or have fallen down. Paul explains, "In a favorable time [God] listened to you, and in a day of salvation [God] . . . helped you" (6:2). Paul gleaned this encouragement from God's promise in Isaiah 49:8–10, 13:

> In a time of favor I have answered you; in a day of salvation I have helped you; I will keep you and give you as a covenant to the people . . . [to say] "Come out," to those who are in darkness . . . they shall not hunger or thirst, neither scorching wind nor sun shall strike them . . . Sing for joy, O heavens, and exult, O earth . . . For the LORD has comforted his people and will have compassion on his afflicted.

Because God favored you as his child, answered you, and helped you in your race of faith, he invites you to extend his favor to other fallen or discouraged runners along the way. Are you prepared to pause in order to extend the Lord's compassionate hand of mercy to another runner? Are you looking to lock arms and partner with both the strong and the weary and to jog together in order to uphold one another as Christ so selflessly did for you?

Words of godly encouragement aren't intended solely for your benefit—they have the chance to lift up other downcast runners and to offer refreshment to the hearts of the weary along the way.

As we conclude the discussion on finding better encouragement, I want to invite you to pause and consider your fellow runners. Who runs beside you? Imagine their names and their faces. Do the people you consider your teammates love and follow Jesus and run the race with endurance? Are you familiar with their trials and weaknesses? Ask the Lord to give you eyes to see the teammates he has called you to run beside. Are your Christian brothers and sisters your competitors? Or are they fellow runners, worthy of receiving better encouragement?

Christian, we must never become so preoccupied with measuring our own spiritual gain or tracking our own forward progress that we "neglect such a great salvation" (Heb. 2:3) and fail to provide good to others. When we are encouraged by the God of encouragement, we will desire to share with our team members the living water of better encouragement that overflows from the abundance of Christ's riches.

God's people are important members of his team; we run together with our eyes faithfully fixed on Jesus. We must prepare, strategize, train, and discipline ourselves to run toward the finish line together. This is the best way to encourage and strengthen one another. We are best equipped to see, encourage, and care for the runners whose paths we regularly cross. Have we made room in our hearts and our schedules to encourage these friends or neighbors as we are able? "We who are strong have an obligation to bear with the failings of the weak, and not to please ourselves" (Rom. 15:1). Ask the Lord to give you opportunities to notice the needs of others and to provide the refreshment of God's better encouragement.

Many of our churches are filled with runners who are weary, thirsty, and have fallen down. When these athletes accidentally chug a mouthful of sand because they've been led away by the promises of a pretty mirage, better encouragement guides these fellow runners back to living water. The church needs runners who are equipped to be patient with the weary as they stumble, gentle as they lead the thirsty to the well that won't run dry, faithful in linking arms to make it to the finish line, and joyful in the hope of celebrating together as victors. Christians aren't designed to run alone. When we run together, we encourage one another to endure.

Paul writes in 2 Corinthians 4:16–18 that Christians

do not lose heart. Though our outer self is wasting away, our inner self is being renewed day by day. For this light momentary affliction is preparing for us an eternal weight of glory beyond all comparison, as we look not to the things that are seen but to the things that are unseen. For the things that are seen are transient, but the things that are unseen are eternal.

When we run together, we are able to help each other see what is good and true, and together we can stay the course of faithfulness. Hebrews 12:1–2 says,

Since we are surrounded by so great a cloud of witnesses, let us also lay aside every weight, and sin which clings so closely, and let us run with endurance the race that is set before us, looking to Jesus, the founder and perfecter of our faith, who for the joy that was set before him endured the cross, despising the shame, and is seated at the right hand of the throne of God.

Your life is one of many encouraging witnesses. You have been joined together with the people of God in order to encourage others today, tomorrow, and possibly for years or generations to come. Through your words of encouragement, you have the opportunity to labor for the kingdom and to join in the work of building up the church. Christ's team of runners must represent him. By running together, the strength of our collective voice becomes louder, beckoning to Christians who lag behind and testifying to unbelieving onlookers. Our unified, steady strides and our eagerness to care for one another are a strong and notable testimony to others. When we run with our eyes fixed on the will of the Father, he will give us eyes to see the people in our path and his Spirit will give us words of grace to encourage them.

While the majority of this book is written to provide Christians with a better and clearer understanding of God's encouragement, receiving encouragement for yourself shouldn't be your end goal. God provides his people with better encouragement and a longer-lasting source of hope so that you will go and encourage those around you. He strengthens his people one by one in order to strengthen his church. By encouraging you, God equips you to run, to endure, and to encourage his entire team to victory.

## Today's Viral Message of Encouragement

As we work to follow the instruction of 1 Thessalonians 4:18 to "encourage one another with these words," we must make sure that we know *which* words Paul meant. One of the ways Christian women can faithfully build each other up in love is by cautiously protecting one another from messages that aren't good, true, or biblical, even when they're marketed to Christians or claim to be encouragement. Before we click, like, or share, let's get in the habit of stopping to consider if Scripture would confirm that the message we like is actually true, honorable, just, pure, lovely, commendable, excellent, or praiseworthy.

When the YouTube video "Who Are You? A Message to All Women" began to make the rounds all over social media, weary and discouraged women clicked, liked, and shared the message with their friends.[3] The short, three-and-a-half-minute video featured a handsome young actor dramatically lit by stage lighting and standing center stage in an empty auditorium as he spoke his impassioned motivational monologue. Looking straight into the camera he aimed to compliment, affirm, inspire, and motivate women with these popular, ear-tickling words: "You are beautiful. You are smart. You are funny. You are kind . . . You are never too much. You are always enough . . . You deserve someone who would give up their life for you because you are powerful, strong, and capable."[4]

As the music grew in intensity, the speaker confidently highlighted women from the Bible. But then he took scriptural stories meant for encouragement and bent and fashioned them into the image of self-help:

> Read the Bible . . . women like Esther, Ruth, Martha, and Mary . . . changed the world forever. Inside every one of you

3    Jon Jorgenson, "Who You Are: A Message to All Women," July 18, 2013, YouTube video, https://youtube.com/.
4    Jorgenson, "Who You Are," 00:24–1:00, 2:10–2:20.

is a woman with the same power, the same strength, and the same world-changing capability, and it's your responsibility to find that woman inside yourself and to set her free . . . This is who you are.[5]

Because he communicated biblical stories and some biblical truth, not every viewer may have caught the self-empowerment framework since some of the words did feel encouraging and refreshing: "I am a daughter of the living God, cherished, loved, and adored above all things by the Creator of all things, for the glory of him who is greater than all things."[6] All of these words were good and true. But the most dangerous part of the message was his closing takeaway: "I am awesome."[7]

We want this to be true. And because we long to be awesome like God, the thesis of this message of encouragement appeals strongly to thirsty spiritual runners. But better self-confidence isn't the message of encouragement that Jesus would have poured into these women. When women are crippled by their own self-doubt and hamstrung by their lack of hope, they long to be led to the living water that refreshes them in Christ. By offering women messages that only aimed to make them feel better, this man had handed all ten million women a piping hot cup of sand as refreshment.

The most important need of discouraged women is not self-confidence but a confident assurance of their identity in Christ. To encourage women in their spiritual adoption, we must be

5  Jorgenson, "Who You Are," 2:22–2:45.
6  Jorgenson, "Who You Are," 2:54–3:06.
7  Jorgenson, "Who You Are," 3:07–3:11.

able to rightly handle the word in the areas of what is truly good and commendable and what is not. When Scripture says, "none is righteous, no not one" (Rom 3:10) and our response is, "Yes, but you are awesome," this does not encourage women to flee sin and cling to righteousness. We need both truth and grace to encourage one another as "iron sharpens iron" (Prov. 27:17). When Paul instructs Christians to "encourage one another with these words" in 1 Thessalonians 4:18, he is referring to the good news that Christ will return and gather his people together to live with him forever. On the day of Christ's return, do we really want our salvation and eternal comfort to be based on whether or not we are awesome?

Romans 15:4 says whatever was written for us in the former days was written so that "through endurance and through the encouragement of the Scriptures we might have hope." And then, verses 5 and 6 ask for God's blessing so that his people would be unified in one singular voice of praise: "May the God of endurance and encouragement grant you to live in such harmony with one another, in accord with Christ Jesus, that together you may with one voice glorify the God and Father of our Lord Jesus Christ."

The church's message of encouragement is one of unity. When we encourage one another, we should aim for the unity of encouragement that grants us to "live in such harmony with one another" that we may glorify Christ with one voice. When we encourage by the same message of promise and gospel grace, we work together to fight for the integrity and purity of the gospel message and witness. When Christians encourage one another through Christ, we work together to "guard the deposit" and "avoid the irreverent babble and contradictions of what is falsely called knowledge" (1 Tim. 6:20).

## Encouraged to Work

In today's busy culture, Christians often fail to encourage one another along the road because we are either unaware, overcommitted, or distracted. Encouraging others often feels like hard work; we're afraid of adding more. But when God places his Spirit in our hearts, he calls us to work for one another with joy (2 Cor. 1:24). In 1 Thessalonians 2 Paul writes, "For you remember, brothers, our labor and toil: we worked night and day, that we might not be a burden to any of you, while we proclaimed to you the gospel of God. . . . For you know how, like a father with his children, we exhorted each one of you and encouraged you" (2:9, 11). As Paul teaches, trains, and instructs the believers, his words of admonition aren't biting or gruff, like an irritated track coach barking at the runners to pick up the pace. Paul writes with the demeanor of a loving father who delights in his responsibility because it benefits those he loves.

In 2 Corinthians 7:3 Paul calls Christians to make room in their hearts for one another, "to die together and to live together." Paul took time to be physically present with the Corinthians and to know their joys, sorrows, and struggles. As he made room in his daily life to get to know and understand the hearts of those he was ministering to, God enabled him to act with great boldness while he taught, encouraged, and exhorted. Paul had a front row seat as the people grew and took pride in their maturing faith and their earnestness in the sight of God (7:12). When the people Paul encouraged then encouraged one another, the encouragement produced spiritual growth, maturity, and energy, which Paul was able to observe in the joy of Titus, whose spirit had been refreshed (7:13).

We must labor together through our own weakness while also being patient with the weakness of others. Hebrews 12:12–14 exhorts runners to "lift [their] drooping hands and strengthen [their] weak knees, and make straight paths for [their] feet, so that what is lame may not be put out of joint but rather be healed. Strive for peace with everyone, and for the holiness without which no one will see the Lord." We work to discipline ourselves in godliness, training and strengthening our faith by the help of the Spirit, because we do not want our own weakness to hinder or harm other runners. We work to encourage others, extending help and healing, with a spirit of peace and restoration.

Colaborers who love one another and work to encourage one another will do so as they have the opportunity; we "do good to everyone, and especially to those who are of the household of faith" (Gal. 6:10). As we make room in our hearts in order to encourage one another, we will be strengthened and encouraged by other saints. But when our daily lives, our schedules, and our circle of friends are too full, we may overlook chances to stop and attend to the needs of others. We must often add margin to our day in order to add encouragement to the lives of those we love. Start close to home. Ask the Lord to grant you opportunities to encourage the people gathered around your dinner table or who sit near you at work or in church. As you encourage others in the goodness of God, your heart will be refreshed. God's people find joy in cheering each other on.

How is the Spirit calling you to become a better encourager? Is he prompting you to pay closer attention to the needs of others? Or to speak up more frequently? How might you listen sacrificially or lovingly exhort? As you consider the members of your local church, which brothers or sisters is the Spirit prompting you to work to encourage? Start today by making a plan to encourage someone God places on your heart in the coming week.

## Encouraged to Commend

While encouragement takes effort, it is a joyful responsibility to refresh God's people. It may be tempting to encourage the people we love by only telling them about ourselves, our own experiences, or our own creative solutions, but better encouragement aims to provide biblical truth that's available and applicable to all of God's people even when their personal experiences and circumstances differ. In other words, strive to avoid making your words and experiences the bulk of your encouragement; let it rather be filled with God's wisdom and counsel. When we elevate our own ideas and solutions above the certain truth of God, we often place additional stumbling blocks on the paths meant to guide the weary and wounded to Jesus. Instead of commending ourselves to others like the Corinthian church in 2 Corinthians 3:1–3, we can help others by commending them to Jesus.

To commend is to present something as suitable or praiseworthy. In Scripture, to commend means "to set together" or "to set one person or thing with another by way of presenting and commending."[8] Vine's *Expository Dictionary* explains that "the saints at Corinth had 'approved themselves in everything to be

8   *Blue Letter Bible*, "παρατίθημι," accessed November 19, 2021, https://www.blueletter bible.org/.

pure.'"[9] They thought they were praiseworthy, so they presented themselves as such, commending themselves to others.

When we primarily encourage others only by our own words, thoughts, or ideas that are not backed by promises in Scripture, we stand to commend God's people to ourselves or to the world's encouragements rather than to God's promises or the good news of Jesus. We must not attempt to solve peoples' problems by commending them to our favorite brands or by selling them products or supplements we think will change their life. We must work harder to commend others to the work of God, even when that means that we feel helpless or have very little to do with providing immediate comfort or solutions. When we commend others to the compassionate care of God, we can trust his grace will provide everything they need through Christ Jesus.

No celebrity-endorsed system will sustain those who were built to be strengthened by the Savior. Followers of Jesus don't commend one another to impotent idols. When we praise and approve what is neither pure nor worthy, we behave like fierce wolves sneaking into God's flock and speaking twisted things to draw away the disciples (Acts 20:29–30). Instead, we must work as ministers of grace, diligently commending the wandering sheep to the word of truth and drawing them back to the safety of the shepherd.

### Encouraged to Build Up

God calls his people to encourage one another in order to build them up in the word of his grace. Throughout the Old and New Testament, as God's people commend one another to the goodness

---

9   *Blue Letter Bible*, "approve," accessed November 19, 2021, https://www.blueletter bible.org/.

of God by regularly speaking, writing, reading, and repeating the words and promises of God, they encourage one another and build each other up, specifically in their knowledge and understanding of God. Psalm 145:4 declares, "One generation shall commend your works to another, and shall declare your mighty acts." Parents who love Jesus are called to teach and train their children in the ways of faith, exhorting them in gospel truth. We encourage our children by praising and commending them to God's truth and beauty demonstrated in Scripture and through all of creation.

Inside our local churches, all of the pastors, shepherds, teachers, and church members labor together to make disciples and equip and encourage each other to faithfully follow Christ toward spiritual maturity. Over time, as we are steadily commended to God and led by his Spirit, God builds and matures our faith. As God strengthens his people, he strengthens his church; together we are better prepared to stand firm.

In Acts 11:23–24 when the good news of the gospel made its way to the church in Jerusalem and Barnabas was sent to Antioch to encourage the new believers, he "came and saw the grace of God, he was glad, and he exhorted them all to remain faithful to the Lord with steadfast purpose . . . And a great many people were added to the Lord." The new believers were encouraged and Barnabas was encouraged. Everyone's faith was strengthened and built up. And God's kingdom grew in number and strength. Barnabas exhorted the Christians to remain faithful by encouraging them to stand firm in Christ. This was *parakaleō* encouragement, "to call to one's side for the purpose of encouragement."[10]

10  *Blue Letter Bible*, "παρακαλέω," accessed September 1, 2021, https://www.blueletter bible.org/.

Acts 11:26 reports that for a whole year Barnabas and Paul drew near, meeting with the church and teaching a great many people. One Sabbath day in Antioch as they read from the Law and the Prophets, they received a message from the rulers of the synagogue saying this: "Brothers, if you have any word of encouragement for the people, say it" (Acts 13:15). By being present and at work among the new believers, Paul and Barnabas were even able to encourage a group of religious scoffers with the truth of the gospel. Paul and Barnabas's word of encouragement was the simple message of Christ's forgiveness and salvation (Acts 11:16–39). As servants of Jesus, their speech displayed that they believed the gospel was a better encouragement.

The true followers of Jesus responded to Paul's message in Acts 13:42–44 with the faith and fruit of gospel encouragement:

> As they went out, [God's] people *begged* that these things might be told [to] them the next Sabbath. And after the meeting . . . many Jews and devout converts to Judaism followed Paul and Barnabas, who, as they spoke with them, urged them to continue in the grace of God. The next Sabbath almost the whole city gathered to hear the word of the Lord.

When God encouraged his people, they were refreshed, but they still thirsted for more of his mercy!

Paul and Barnabas took every opportunity to encourage and build up the church, even at great risk to their own safety, because they understood and valued the work that the Holy Spirit had set them apart for and called them to (Acts 13:2). Their lives were a testimony of faithful endurance and obedience because they weren't sidelined by weakness or adversity—they encouraged themselves in the Lord and trusted God's power to exhort, encourage, and build up all who had spiritual ears to hear. As we evangelize, teach, and encourage, God builds his church because he is committed to preserving his name and glory and ensuring his praise spreads across the globe and spans all ages. God's plan of encouragement works strategically to carry his hope to every runner, every team, and every nation as he builds us into a people for his own possession and praise.

### Run to Rejoice

Take heart, weary and discouraged runner—Christ runs with you. He will encourage you and lift you up. He will strengthen you, protect you, and guide you with his righteous right hand. You don't need to be awesome or impressive to be a part of his team or a member of his family. You need only trust and believe that he is your salvation and hope. Apart from him, you have no better encouragement, promised good, power, strength, comfort, or hope.

God will strengthen you for endurance while you labor alongside his family as an important and contributing member of the team. He has called and equipped pastors, teachers, mentors, friends, disciples, and church members to run beside you for your encouragement and for your sanctification and strength. Rejoice and give thanks for those who exhort you through the encouragement of God's word as they teach, reprove, correct, and train you for righteousness, that you may be complete, equipped for every good work (2 Tim. 3:16–17).

Encourage the weak, weary, and fainthearted at every mile marker along the way. Gather together. Be physically present with one another without the interruptive glow of your phone screen. Meet together to discuss struggles and victories. Pray together about everything, not just the comfortable subjects. Text each other Scriptures filled with hope and promise. Strive to speak and type words of life-giving exhortation. When a friend is in a wilderness season, look for the fruit and point out the proof of God's provision. Get in the habit of commending one another to God's promises of provision. Be willing to wait patiently together for his blessings. Check in on the weak and weary long after the phone calls and casserole deliveries have ended.

Sister, the change starts with you. As we conclude I want to invite you to pause and humbly ask God to encourage and strengthen *you* in order to build his church and glorify his name. God will form and shape you into his instrument of better encouragement in order to carry his name (Acts 9:15). Ask God to give you the courage and confidence of Paul and Barnabas, that you might offer better, gospel-centered encouragement to others. Pray that the Spirit would give you eyes to see and words to rejoice as God encourages you and builds up his saints. Look for the fruit of his Spirit and point it out for the encouragement of others. And finally, pray for your own local church and ask God to show you how you might become a source of better encouragement to your pastors and fellow church members.

Christ will effectively stimulate, hearten, and urge you forward by his perfect strength; he is God's better promise, given for you, so that you can endure with hope in the reward of resurrection. What better encouragement could you ask for than this?

Be strong. Christ is the forerunner, running at the front and center of the crowd of faithful witnesses. Take heart. He knows every path and every curve of the race set before you. Do not fear. He is able to strengthen weak knees. Come and drink. He will refresh you with the living water that never runs dry. Stand firm. He will help you endure to the finish line and perfectly establish you as a victorious finisher in the final day. Rejoice. You never run alone. You are better encouraged through Christ.

# A Note on Building a Culture of Encouragement in Your Church

*"And we urge you . . . admonish the idle,*
*encourage the fainthearted, help the weak,*
*be patient with them all" (1 Thess. 5:14)*

IN THE TWENTY YEARS my husband and I have been married, we've had the pleasure of being a part of several different church families: the tiny one in our college town, a small rural one after we graduated, a bigger one in Houston, and now the church we planted in Baltimore, Maryland. At each of these churches, I entered the church community as a woman who loved Jesus and desired to grow in spiritual maturity and fruitfully contribute to our new church. But I also entered each of these families weary and heavy laden with wounds, sin, and baggage. In each and every stage of life and spiritual maturity level, no matter what age my children were or how busy I was with ministry responsibilities, I've always valued encouragement within the body of Christ.

In each church, I remember the encouragers. Janet. Gayle. Debbie. Sandra. Pauline. Tom. Dee. Nona. Mike. Kari. Nancy. Renee. These are only a few. The list could go on and on and on. The encouragers who impacted me the most were the ones whose lives were a demonstration of the fruit of the Spirit. Their lives breathed encouragement because they were filled with joy. These men and women gently helped me see, understand, and apply the promises of God when my heart was weary. Their words and demonstrations of God's kindness helped me to be strong, stand firm, and take heart in various seasons of discouragement. My faith, my testimony, and my work are stronger today because of the encouragement of these saints.

Some pastors and teachers are naturally gifted encouragers. For others, it takes time and effort. Churches are filled with members who all have different gifts. Whether or not your church members joyfully encourage with the skill of Barnabas or Paul, every church has room to grow in how we equip each member for the ongoing responsibility of encouraging one another.

Inside the church, encouragement can be somewhat of a cultural phenomenon—and I mean this in a good way. Church members (and therefore the larger culture they contribute to) are able to shift, change, grow, and mature when they are led and guided by God's word and by gentle shepherds. Years ago when my husband was on staff at a larger church in Houston, a visitor to our church later referred to us as "freakishly friendly." Most people took this as a compliment. The comment surprised no one because we all knew it to be true. Our church body was freakishly friendly because most of us learned it from our pastors who were freakishly friendly. This particular designation became somewhat of a positive identifying mark of distinction.

What is your church known for? Where is there already evidence of the fruit of the Spirit at work? As you brainstorm how you might work to cultivate a culture of encouragement, consider the unique personality of your church and how it has been shaped and defined over the years by the diligent contributions of certain leaders or church members. When God's people bring their desires, abilities, strengths, gifts, and resources to the church and work for his glory, God produces beautiful fruit!

Here are just a few ideas and thoughts to consider if you are hoping to foster a culture of encouragement inside your own local church:

- **Be encouraged.** Ask the Lord to change your heart through the power of his word and Spirit. Seek to be encouraged by his word daily. Read the Psalms. Sing songs of praise. Write in a prayer journal. Make a habit of meditating on the encouragement of God's truth throughout your day.
- **Encouragement begins with prayer.** Like any work of God, commit your plans to the Lord and ask for him to fill the church with encouragers who are discerning in the word of truth, protective of the purity of the gospel, committed to the maturity of God's people, and filled with the fruit of the Spirit.
- **Model biblical encouragement in your own life and relationships.** Start with the people inside your own household. Expand to your closest friends. Don't feel the need to start anything official. Change your own habits first.
- **Encouragement doesn't need to be programmatic.** You may be the one God has called to start investing in a ministry of

encouragement first. Start small. While it doesn't need to be programmatic, you can aim to strategize how you and a few friends might encourage a specific group of people. Who could you encourage? You don't need a committee or a leadership team; just invest in others relationally.

- **Encouragement is a learned skill.** Just like other parts of discipleship, encouragement should be taught, practiced, and replicated as an important aspect of the Christian faith. Encouragement is Spirit dependent. Ask God to show you who you might encourage. Pray for the Spirit's wisdom and that he would provide the good counsel of a well-timed word. Depend on the Spirit to do the work of empowerment. You are the messenger not the Spirit.

- **Encourage regularly and systematically.** Once you decide who God has called you to encourage, privately commit to their ongoing encouragement; this might include checking in on them each Sunday, praying once a week, or even sending a text whenever you hear there's an extra need. Choose to invest for the long haul, even if it means only making small relational investments over time. You may be surprised at how God is able to support someone through simple words of truth.

- **Encouragement multiplies.** Consider getting together with a small group of friends just for the purpose of encouragement and prayer. Keep the time short and simple. Start with a specified start and end date. You can always recommit once you're finished. Your time together doesn't need to be a production. You might prioritize one area to pray for encouragement: spiritual disciplines, family, friendships, work, physical health, or something else. Find and discuss a Scripture to meditate on or pray for one another throughout the week. If this seems too complicated, you could always spend the time pairing up to check in on and pray for one another during the week; just keep the focus on encouragement. Then, share the blessing of encouragement by breaking out of your group, multiplying, and making new groups that include additional women.

- **Commit to studying encouragement together.** If you want to go deeper in discussing biblical encouragement with a group in your church, you could start by studying the subject of encouragement in Scripture. Alternatively, you could study the life of Jesus, Barnabas, or Paul. Or, you could always read through this book.

- **Be patient as you work and pray for change.** A church's culture doesn't take shape overnight. As you work to implement a culture of encouragement, be patient and diligent in studying encouragement with church members. Be patient with the weak who may struggle to biblically encourage. Be patient with those who aren't skilled in blessing others with their words. Celebrate small, steady, incremental changes when you notice them.

- **Encourage the weak.** If you're not sure who to encourage, ask your pastor or a ministry leader. Share your desire to grow in the skill of encouragement and ask them for ideas. Pastors and ministry directors are often aware of church members who could use an extra friend or a voice of support.

- **Encourage your pastor.** Ministry is tough. And even if your pastor or ministry leader seems strong, they are shouldering heavy burdens. Look for ways to exhort and encourage the shepherds God has given you. Point out glimpses of fruit in their lives. Thank them for their sacrificial living and ask how you might pray for their strength and endurance. Celebrate fruit in their ministry whenever you can. Share openly with them when you notice fruit or growth in your own life that is the result of their ministry. Give your leaders the opportunity to celebrate and rejoice with you.

- **Encourage your church.** Pray for your pastors, elders, and teachers to be strengthened by grace through the encouraging words and actions of the church's members. Pray and ask the Lord for wisdom and humility to discern how God might use you to encourage and strengthen others within your own local church.

*A friendly word of advice from a pastor's wife: Don't cast a broader vision to the church for a new ministry endeavor without speaking privately to your pastors, staff, or elders. Be considerate of the church's ministry structure and bring your ideas humbly to the leaders God has entrusted with your shepherding. If you are considering approaching a pastor or leader, make sure you ask them for their feedback. Would they recognize and affirm you as an encourager? Would others? If you aren't sure, seek honest feedback from your spouse, a family member, a close friend, or a trusted ministry leader about whether you would be a good fit for heading up a discussion or a group based on encouragement. Any time you are considering teaching or leading God's people in the study of his word, make sure that people who are familiar with your character, spiritual maturity, and fruit would affirm your desire seems good and pleasing to the Lord.

# A Note on Depression and Mental Illness

WHEN DISCOURAGEMENT IMPACTS your physical, emotional, or mental well-being, it may need to be addressed on a deeper level than this book is intended to cover. I am not a medical doctor or a therapist but a sister with a word of caution. It is wise to seek the help of a medical professional while also working to rest in God's encouragement and promises.

Christians often feel vulnerable and insecure in discerning when and how to address emotional and mental health concerns with answers that venture outside the bounds of prayer, Bible reading, and fellowship in the local church. But sometimes, sufferers need additional outside support to adequately understand what's going on inside the heart and inside the body. As I write to women who are reading about discouragement, I am hyperaware that out of all of the weak and weary saints battling discouragement, some bring an additional weight of suffering into an already difficult battle. My heart is particularly tender toward sufferers who may be battling clinical depression, postpartum depression, or other mood disorders, whether or not they've ever been diagnosed or treated for one.

As Christians, we live aware of our spiritual health, but sometimes we can be tempted to overlook the fact that as human beings we are also embodied souls who must responsibly steward our physical, mental, and emotional health. Our daily lives are easily impacted by physical and environmental factors that are both inside and outside of our control. We see the effect on our energy levels when we don't eat or sleep. We may clench our shoulders or grind our teeth when we're stressed. We must live with the awareness of how our own physical body responds to emotional and mental stress and know when we need additional help or support to address feelings of sadness or depression that won't go away, increase in intensity or frequency, or negatively impact daily life. Your struggle may be more than just discouragement.

In women, depression is a common occurrence, and Christian women must not immediately rule out the possibility or dismiss it as purely a spiritual concern. The American Psychiatric Association describes depression, or major depressive disorder, as "a common and serious medical illness that negatively affects how you feel, the way you think and how you act," including "feelings of sadness and/or a loss of interest in activities you once enjoyed" and are so intense that they "can decrease your ability to function."[1] Some studies show one third of women will experience a major depressive episode in their lifetime. While you shouldn't jump to conclusions at every sign of trouble or sadness, it helps to know the facts.

1  "What is Depression?" *American Psychiatric Association*, accessed September 1, 2021, https://www.psychiatry.org/.

In his book *Spiritual Depression*, Pastor Martyn Lloyd-Jones asked, "Does someone hold the view that as long as you are a Christian it does not matter what the condition of your body is?"[2] Anyone who believes this will eventually be disillusioned. Physical conditions play a part: "tiredness, overstrain, illness, any form of illness. You cannot isolate the spiritual from the physical for we are body, mind and spirit."[3] Plenty of godly, spiritually mature, faithful followers of Christ have struggled with depression and other mental illnesses throughout the ages. Often clinical depression, mood disorders, and mental health struggles are biological or circumstantial and not the product of a specific indwelling sin pattern. Sometimes, these experiences can be brought on by another person's sin and we need outside help to understand how we've been wounded and how we might begin to heal. In most cases, mental illness is multifaceted.

There are many physical and environmental facts to take into consideration: the biochemistry of brain chemicals, rising and falling hormone levels (especially during puberty, menstruation, pregnancy, postpartum, or menopause), genetics, gut health, thyroid or immune system problems, and vitamin deficiency. Even gloomy weather and cold, dark seasons can negatively impact mental and emotional health! Medical professionals can skillfully assist you in coming to an understanding and accurate diagnosis. Because Christians are embodied souls, they should seek comfort and healing that address matters of the heart, soul, mind, and body.

2  Martyn Lloyd-Jones, *Spiritual Depression: Its Causes and Cures* (London: HarperCollins, 1998), 18–19.
3  Lloyd-Jones, *Spiritual Depression*, 18–19.

If you suspect you might be dealing with depression or some other mental or emotional health problem, start by evaluating and keeping track of any concerning changes in your mood or behavior as well as any new physical symptoms. Are you more fatigued than normal? Do you want to sleep all the time? Has your appetite changed? Have you noticed headaches, an upset stomach, or an increased heart rate? Do you experience frequent mood swings or cry more easily than usual? Take note of any physical symptoms as they could be your body's signs of distress. If your sadness or troubling symptoms last longer than two weeks, it's time to let someone else in on your struggle.

In times of spiritual darkness, it's important to invite outside observation from a person who loves you and is close to you and who can help you stay focused on the broader picture of your emotional and physical well-being, help you distinguish what is good and true when you feel overwhelmed, assist you in decision-making when you're weary, and hold you accountable to taking next steps when you feel too tired to pursue healing. If you are suffering, begin by asking a family member, your spouse, a friend, a ministry leader, or someone who loves you and is physically present in your daily life (as opposed to someone who only sees you online where it's easier to hide feelings) if they've noticed any changes in your mood or behavior. Humbly listen and consider their observations and concerns; they are often able to see your situation with the light of truth that you aren't as able to see when surrounded by clouds of darkness. If they share your concerns or add additional ones, ask them to walk with you through the steps of seeking the help of a medical professional.

You can begin by calling your doctor to make an appointment or you can go straight to a specialist—like a psychologist or psychiatrist—who is uniquely skilled in these specific issues. A skilled doctor will listen to your concerns, ask additional diagnostic questions, and help you gain an accurate understanding or diagnosis. Don't attempt to analyze or diagnose yourself online; leave that to the professionals. Trained doctors are far more capable of determining whether your symptoms require intervention and they will help you evaluate potential treatment plans that may or may not include medication, talk therapy, cognitive behavioral therapy, other therapeutic approaches, or a combination of remedies.

If a doctor diagnoses you with clinical depression or another emotional or mental disorder, your diagnosis need not burden you with the additional weight of spiritual stigma. Your diagnosis is not a commentary on your spiritual maturity or a measure of your faith; it's an illness that draws you closer to your healer for daily mercy. By God's grace, he has provided medical research and skilled physicians who are able to offer sufferers tangible measures of grace that weren't available to depressed Christians who lived in previous centuries. Today, God has granted his people access to an abundance of helpful resources. Mental health problems aren't solved overnight and do not often heal on their own. Surround yourself with people who know what you're struggling with and who are able to provide you with love and support as you heal.

## Questions to Evaluate Troublesome Symptoms

**History:** Is there a history of mental illness or mood disorders in your family? Have you had a previous diagnosis that might indicate you're experiencing another similar episode?

**Intensity:** Do your feelings or emotions seem increasingly irrational, more intense, or more unpredictable than usual? Are you feeling more weepy, irritable, or anxious than you typically feel?

**Duration:** Have your symptoms lasted longer than two weeks? How long have your symptoms been present?

**Disturbance in Your Daily Life:** Have you noticed a change in your ability to function? Are you unable to eat, sleep, or enjoy activities you usually enjoy? Are you struggling to concentrate or make decisions?

**Suicidal Ideations:** If you are contemplating physical injury to yourself, death, or suicide, seek immediate help from an emergency provider.

If you're concerned you might be suffering from depression, don't hesitate to seek the expertise of a medical professional; you can simultaneously seek physical healing *and* the support of your family, your pastor, and your local church.

# Encouraging Scriptures to Memorize

- "For whatever was written in former days was written for our instruction, that through endurance and through the encouragement of the Scriptures we might have hope." (Rom. 15:4)
- "May the God of endurance and encouragement grant you to live in such harmony with one another, in accord with Christ Jesus, that together you may with one voice glorify the God and Father of our Lord Jesus Christ." (Rom. 15:5–6)
- "And we urge you . . . admonish the idle, encourage the fainthearted, help the weak, be patient with them all." (1 Thess. 5:14)
- "I believe that I shall look upon the goodness of the LORD in the land of the living!" (Ps. 27:13)
- "It is good for me that I was afflicted, that I might learn your statutes." (Ps. 119:71)
- "Be strong and courageous. Do not fear or be in dread of them, for it is the LORD your God who goes with you. He will not leave you or forsake you." (Deut. 31:6)

- "Do not be frightened, and do not be dismayed, for the LORD your God is with you wherever you go." (Josh. 1:9)
- "When the poor and needy seek water, and there is none, and their tongue is parched with thirst, I the LORD will answer them; I the God of Israel will not forsake them." (Isa. 41:17)
- "Jesus turned, and seeing her he said, 'Take heart, daughter; your faith has made you well.' And instantly the woman was made well." (Matt. 9:22)
- "On the last day of the feast, the great day, Jesus stood up and cried out, 'If anyone thirsts, let him come to me and drink.'" (John 7:37)
- "I have said these things to you, that in me you may have peace. In the world you will have tribulation. But take heart; I have overcome the world." (John 16:33)
- "And I was with you in weakness and in fear and much trembling, and my speech and my message were not in plausible words of wisdom, but in demonstration of the Spirit and of power, so that your faith might not rest in the wisdom of men but in the power of God." (1 Cor. 2:3–5)
- "But I do not account my life of any value nor as precious to myself, if only I may finish my course and the ministry that I received from the Lord Jesus, to testify to the gospel of the grace of God." (Acts 20:24)
- "Therefore, since we are surrounded by so great a cloud of witnesses, let us also lay aside every weight, and sin which clings so closely, and let us run with endurance the race that is set before us, looking to Jesus, the founder and perfecter of our faith, who for the joy that was set before him endured

the cross, despising the shame, and is seated at the right hand of the throne of God." (Heb. 12:1–2)

- "Therefore lift your drooping hands and strengthen your weak knees, and make straight paths for your feet, so that what is lame may not be put out of joint but rather be healed." (Heb. 12:12–13)
- "Blessed be the God and Father of our Lord Jesus Christ! According to his great mercy, he has caused us to be born again to a living hope through the resurrection of Jesus Christ from the dead, to an inheritance that is imperishable, undefiled, and unfading, kept in heaven for you." (1 Pet. 1:3–4)
- "All Scripture is breathed out by God and profitable for teaching, for reproof, for correction, and for training in righteousness, that the man of God may be complete, equipped for every good work." (2 Tim. 3:16–17)
- "And let us not grow weary of doing good, for in due season we will reap, if we do not give up. So then, as we have opportunity, let us do good to everyone, and especially to those who are of the household of faith." (Gal. 6:9–10)
- "No unbelief made him waver concerning the promise of God, but he grew strong in his faith as he gave glory to God." (Rom. 4:20)

# Acknowledgments

THE ONLY PROPER WAY to conclude a book on encouragement is to acknowledge as many of the encouragers as I can who have quietly sustained, uplifted, and strengthened me to do the work set before me. When I felt like a mumbling Moses, God encouraged me to stand, find his grace, and walk by faith through the wilderness. Here are just a few tangible demonstrations of the Lord's provision.

My husband Kyle emboldens me to "just keep writing." By making room for me to serve the Lord inside and outside our home, Kyle regularly encourages me to pursue ministry opportunities that will allow me to dream and create but also challenge and stretch me, while filling me with joy and wonder that leads me to worship God. I'm so thankful to have the chance to grow and be sanctified together as we continually learn to see with the light of truth and extend each other the grace we often need help finding for ourselves.

My kids anchor and lift me. My daughter Madeline encourages me to grow as a writer, to continually commit to the craft, honing my creativity and skills. And then there's my four sons.

Collin's thoughtfulness and generosity encourage me in weariness; he's always ready with a listening ear, a hug, and an afternoon cup of coffee. Jude's sheer enjoyment of life regularly encourages me to smile, joke, laugh, play, and eat good food. Spencer's quiet reservation reminds me that there is often good fruit in stillness and quietness; those who think deeply and speak slowly often listen more closely, ask better questions, and gain a heart of wisdom. Rex is the gift of laughter that I didn't know I needed, teaching me to parent with greater peace and gentleness and to enjoy the messiness of the process. Kids, you are all my favorite.

All of my local church ladies spur me on to good works by encouraging me with their words, prayers, and questions. I could not and would not be able to do any of this work in the church at large if I weren't seen and known by each of them. In all my tears and weakness, they have walked me through the woods (some of them more literally than others), asked insightful questions, attentively listened, and inspired me to trust God's grace would be present in each step. I am immeasurably thankful to all my K's (Kari, Karen, Kelsey, and Renee' K) and to Jen, Sharon, Nancy, Dorothy, and the two Elizabeths for their loyalty and sacrificial service, for watching kids and dogs, and for providing meals, ceaseless prayers, and words of wisdom and grace.

In the absence of any living grandparents of my own, the Lord kindly provided me with an adopted grandmother in Nancy Bach who generously opened her home to me as a quiet writing sanctuary. By insisting I turn on the fan to avoid heatstroke, wear her coat to avoid the chill, and put on shoes to avoid injuring my bare feet on the acorn-covered deck, and by ensuring I remained hydrated and well-fed, she nourished and sustained me. Nancy encourages me to see the fullness of my life as the evidence of God's abundant blessing and to continue working from a heart of gratitude.

In a season of pain and suffering, God provided healers whose words have administered deep grace to my soul. He provided Maria Garriott who selflessly reached out and invited me into her home where she's cultivated a safe place for ministry wives to talk, breathe, laugh, and cry together. I am grateful to have a wise and talented local writer friend who generously mentors me in all things ministry, mothering, and marriage. Through Maria, God provided Becky LoPicollo (BeLoPeLo) who is the seven to my three, who goes before me and then tells me how to do things, who laughs with me when that's all that's left to do, and who celebrates me when I'm too awkward to know how to celebrate life's victories. And I owe a debt of gratitude to Kim Sütter for skillfully holding up a mirror to my soul without scaring me away and teaching me how to see and comprehend the depth and the mercy of Christ. What grace and truth these women carry to others.

In the days when living far from home weighed heavily, God encouraged our family through our parents' love, support, and generosity. Their willingness to pray for us, fly to us, and host our large and energetic family ensured we remained physically and emotionally well during the difficulty of pandemic living. At forty years old, we still need your encouragement. I certainly wouldn't have finished this book (or broken my collarbone or caught COVID) without your support during the infamous summer 2021 trip to Texas. To my "little" brother David, his wife Megan, and his girls, thank you for investing time and energy into strengthening our family, especially since we moved across the country. And thank you to the friends who've become family. Alissa, Julia, Gretchen, and Renee' M, you each faithfully stand as evergreen encouragers when I'm lost in the forest.

Thank you to the writers who remind me that writing isn't a vain hobby but a useful skill for building into the kingdom. You encourage me to labor with intentionality, consistency, and hope, knowing that in due time our work will produce a harvest of righteousness. Thank you Megan Hill for your friendship, for indulging my distracted texting antics, and for skillfully wielding both the red pen and the words of life. You regularly strengthen the weak-hearted. Thank you Melissa Kruger, Courtney Doctor, and Jen Wilkin for the ways you've publicly and privately encouraged me over the years and for continually paving the way for women to teach God's word. Thank you to the entire team at Crossway for your enthusiasm and excellence.

When church planting felt impossible, God provided ministry supporters who encouraged us with their letters, calls, prayers, financial support, and gracious acts of service. God regularly utilizes your generosity to show me, my husband, and our children that we are not in this world or this ministry alone.

To all those who've taught me, been patient with me, and faithfully encouraged me, thank you. God has used your words and actions to strengthen me for marriage, motherhood, ministry, and more. Each of you are good gifts that bind me closer to Jesus and beckon me to bless and encourage others more and more with each new day.

# General Index

# Scripture Index

# TGC THE GOSPEL COALITION

**The Gospel Coalition (TGC)** supports the church in making disciples of all nations, by providing gospel-centered resources that are trusted and timely, winsome and wise.

Guided by a Council of more than 40 pastors in the Reformed tradition, TGC seeks to advance gospel-centered ministry for the next generation by producing content (including articles, podcasts, videos, courses, and books) and convening leaders (including conferences, virtual events, training, and regional chapters).

In all of this we want to help Christians around the world better grasp the gospel of Jesus Christ and apply it to all of life in the 21st century. We want to offer biblical truth in an era of great confusion. We want to offer gospel-centered hope for the searching.

Through its women's initiatives, The Gospel Coalition aims to support the growth of women in faithfully studying and sharing the Scriptures; in actively loving and serving the church; and in spreading the gospel of Jesus Christ in all their callings.

Join us by visiting TGC.org so you can be equipped to love God with all your heart, soul, mind, and strength, and to love your neighbor as yourself.

**TGC.org**

# Also Available from the Gospel Coalition

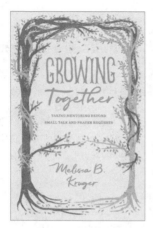
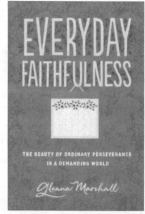

For more information, visit **crossway.org**.